Gourmet's
In·Short·Order

RECIPES IN 45 MINUTES OR LESS *AND* EASY MENUS

Gourmet's In·Short·Order

RECIPES IN 45 MINUTES OR LESS *AND* EASY MENUS

From the Editors of Gourmet

◆ ◆ ◆

Photographs by Romulo A. Yanes

CONDÉ NAST BOOKS ◆ RANDOM HOUSE
new york

LIBRARY OF CONGRESS CATALOGING-IN-
PUBLICATION DATA

Gourmet's In Short Order: 250 fabulous recipes in under
forty-five minutes/the editors of Gourmet

   p. cm.
  ISBN 0-679-42745-7
   1. Quick and easy cookery. 2. Menus. I. Gourmet.
TX833.5.G68   1993   644.5'55—dc20   93-1027
                                                  CIP

Some of the recipes in this work were published previously
in Gourmet Magazine.

Manufactured in the United States of America

987654

 Indicates that a recipe can be doubled.

All of the informative text in this book was written by
Diane Keitt and Judith Tropea.

The text of this book was set in Adobe Garamond by the
Composition Department of The Condé Nast Publications
Inc. The four-color separations were done by The Color
Company, Seiple Lithographers, and Applied Graphic
Technologies. The book was printed and bound at R. R.
Donnelley and Sons. Text paper is Citation Webb Gloss.

Front Jacket: "Rack of Lamb with Tarragon Lemon Sauce"
(page 99); "Honey-Glazed Baby Carrots" (page 149);
"Herbed New Potatoes" (page 152).

Back Jacket: "Linguine with Shrimp and Saffron Sauce"
(page 129); "Chocolate Sponge Moons Filled with Peaches
and Cream" (page 179); "Sole Paupiettes with Orange
Rosemary Butter Sauce" (page 74).

Frontispiece: "Chocolate Raspberry Shortcakes" (page 173).

For Condé Nast Books
Jill Cohen, *Vice President*
Ellen Maria Bruzelius, *Direct Marketing Manager*
Kristine Smith-Cunningham, *Advertising Promotion Manager*
Mary Ellen Kelly, *Fulfillment Manager*
Lisa Faith Phillips, *Direct Marketing Associate*
Diane Pesce, *Composition Production Manager*
Serafino J. Cambareri, *Quality Control Manager*

For *Gourmet* Books
Diane Keitt, *Editor*
Judith Tropea, *Associate Editor*

For *Gourmet* Magazine
Gail Zweigenthal, *Editor-in-Chief*

Zanne Early Zakroff, *Executive Food Editor*
Kemp Miles Minifie, *Senior Food Editor*
Alexis M. Touchet, *Associate Food Editor*
Leslie Glover Pendleton, *Food Editor*
Amy Mastrangelo, *Food Editor*
Kathleen Nilon Atencio, *Food Editor*
Lori Longbotham, *Food Editor*
Elizabeth S. Imperatore, *Food Editor*

Romulo A. Yanes, *Photographer*
Marjorie H. Webb, *Stylist*
Nancy Purdum, *Stylist*

Produced in association with
Media Projects Incorporated
Carter Smith, *Executive Editor*
Anne Wright, *Project Editor*
Shelley Latham, *Associate Project Editor*
Marilyn Flaig, *Indexer*
Harakawa Sisco Inc., *Art/Production Director*

ACKNOWLEDGMENTS

Gourmet's *In Short Order* was produced on a very tight schedule with the assistance of many talented people. The editors of *Gourmet* Books would like to thank those colleagues and freelancers who were so helpful throughout the project.

The enthusiasm and creative expertise of Zanne Early Zakroff, *Gourmet's* Executive Food Editor, were instrumental in the development of this cookbook. She skillfully devised all the new, exciting recipes as well as ten outstanding menus that demonstrate how quick fare can be delicious and elegant. Each menu was complemented with beverage selections provided by Gerald Asher, *Gourmet's* Wine Editor.

All the recipes were carefully tested in *Gourmet's* kitchens by members of the food department, including Kemp Miles Minifie (who also styled the food for our jacket), Alexis M. Touchet, Amy Mastrangelo, and Lori Longbotham. Our resourceful freelancer Georgia Chan Downard also helped out with the recipe testing.

Beautiful full-color photographs by Romulo A. Yanes appear throughout the book. All photographs were inventively styled by Marjorie H. Webb and Nancy Purdum, while food-styling was performed by *Gourmet's* food editors.

We would also like to thank Ann Harakawa, our book designer, whose creativity gave this book its unique style. The book is further enhanced by Susan Blubaugh's clever illustrations. And, finally, thanks to Toni Rachiele for her careful proofreading of the recipes and to Rebecca Ynocencio, who answered our editorial queries.

Contents

The Menus 13

The Recipes 35

G *ourmet*'s food is outstanding: in taste, in style, in presentation. But who could possibly take the time to prepare such wonderful fare everyday? With this volume we would like to show you the quick yet elegant side of *Gourmet* cooking that has been attracting our busy readers for quite some time.

We know that the demands of your life mean that you have less time to spend in the kitchen, especially after a long day at work or during a hectic weekend. For nearly a decade *Gourmet*'s In Short Order column has met your special needs with delicious recipes for two that can be prepared in 45 minutes or less. Over the past few years we have received numerous requests from our readers for a collection of these recipes, and now we are happy to present *Gourmet*'s *In Short Order* cookbook.

Here you will find over 100 of your favorite In Short Order recipes and many wonderful additions. Expressly for this book, Zanne Early Zakroff, our Executive Food Editor, has developed over 140 brand-new quick dishes for two. And, to save menu-planning time, she has carefully created ten easy yet special menus for brunch, lunch, and dinner. Menus and recipes that can be doubled to serve four have been indicated (we have even added an index of these dishes). This helpful feature gives you the option to entertain family and friends with ease!

As in our previous books, exquisite *Gourmet* photographs offer valuable table setting and food-styling ideas. With a little know-how and our quick, delicious recipes, you can easily be a gourmet chef every day of the week.

Gail Zweigenthal
Editor-In-Chief

INTRODUCTION

T ime. There never is enough of it these days, especially when it comes to cooking. All too often we turn to fast convenience foods and take-out fare filled with additives and sodium — not a wise way to eat! Now, for all busy cooks, *Gourmet* combines the freshest ingredients and the newest culinary ideas in 250 recipes that can be made in 45 minutes or less. Also, ten simple menus — as elegant as they are easy — are a delightful bonus. Be assured, neither *Gourmet* flavor nor style has been compromised to save those extra minutes in the kitchen.

These dishes are filled with color — shiny red bell peppers, fresh green peas, bright orange carrots... with texture — crisp endive, toasted pine nuts, creamy goat cheese... with fresh herbs — fragrant basil, pungent garlic, refreshing fennel... with spices — sweet cinnamon, piquant gingerroot, blazing-hot chilies... and with condiments — rich Kalamata olives, warm sun-dried tomatoes, tangy mustards.... There is an abundance of tastes and flavors to try.

We begin with the menus — ten delicious contemporary meals include brunches, lunches (these also make nice lighter suppers), and dinners. All serve two persons, but many can be doubled to serve four (look for our doubling symbol ◆4◆ to help you find these menus). The dishes, culled from the recipe section for their outstanding style and flavor, create meals that look and taste much more time-consuming than they really are. You will also notice that we encourage the chef to take certain shortcuts. By all means, fix your own mixed greens salad with your favorite dressing, buy a warm, fresh crusty bread from the local bakery, or slice those luscious tomatoes from the farmer's market for a simple side dish. After all, smart cooks know that superb meals can always be made without a fuss.

The recipe section follows with over two hundred very special quick and easy recipes for two. More than half the recipes are brand-new, and all have been tested in *Gourmet*'s kitchens. There are starters, quick breads and pizzas, soups, fish, shellfish, meat, poultry, cheese dishes, pastas, grains, vegetables, salads, and desserts — all organized by chapter — ready to use in our suggested menus or in your own combinations, perhaps with wonderful leftovers that you already have on hand. Throughout the section, recipes that can be doubled to serve four are indicated (just remember that doubling a recipe will naturally take a bit more time to prepare).

This collection offers a variety of dishes to meet your different needs. When you are running late, for example, turn to recipes that are actually meals-in-one, such as Chicken Roasted with Potatoes, Peppers, and Shallots (*page 107*), or Individual Mushroom, Red Onion, and Arugula Pizzas (*page 54*), or Pasta with Bell Peppers, Goat Cheese, and Basil (*page 165*). Lighter meals might include a bowl of Vegetable and Bacon Chowder (*page 64*), or Green Bean, Swiss Cheese, and Hazelnut Salad (*page 163*); while super-quick snacks on the run can be found in Fried Feta with Orégano Vinaigrette (*page 122*) or Grilled Cheddar, Pear, and Chutney Sandwiches (*page 123*). Of course, soon enough, you will have your own favorites.

To save time in the kitchen, organization is key. First, decide which menu (or group of recipes) you would like to prepare, read through the recipes, and make a shopping list of all the ingredients you will need. Always buy the freshest ingredients and never skimp on quality. Then, before you start cooking, read through each recipe again and decide the order in which you are going to prepare and cook the recipes so that each course will be ready to serve at the right time. Finally, preheat the oven if necessary, prepare and measure out all ingredients, and ready your cooking equipment and utensils.

At the back of this volume you will find two indexes — a general index and an index of recipes that can be doubled — that will help you save time when creating your own menus. And, a list of table setting acknowledgments tells you exactly where to find the items pictured in our photographs.

One final thought: Never tell anyone how quickly you were able to prepare these dishes — let them feel pampered instead. Enjoy!

the menus

Scandinavian Vegetable Soup with Shrimp

A LIGHT
SPRING BRUNCH

Scandinavian Vegetable Soup with Shrimp

64

Cumin Melba Toasts

53

Mixed Greens Salad

Lemon Yogurt Mousse

180

SERVES 2

SCHARZHOFBERGER
RIESLING TROCKEN
1990,
REICHSGRAF
VON KESSELSTATT

Sausage and Grits Frittata; Herbed Boston Lettuce and Cherry Tomato Salad

BRUNCH FOR
A CHILLY WEEKEND

Sausage and Grits Frittata

117

Herbed Boston Lettuce and Cherry Tomato Salad

168

Chili Cornmeal Biscuits

48

Cranberry Pear Cobbler

178

SERVES 2

SAINTSBURY
CARNEROS
PINOT NOIR 1990

Linguine with Shrimp and Saffron Sauce

A ROMANTIC
LUNCH

Asparagus Soup with Tarragon

58

Linguine with Shrimp and Saffron Sauce

129

Mixed Greens Salad

Crusty Bread

STORE-BOUGHT

Almond Tea Cakes

173

SERVES 2

ORVIETO CASTELLO
DELLA SALA 1990,
ANTINORI

Apple Tarts

A RAINY DAY
LUNCH

Braised Chicken with Onions, Bacon, and White Wine

106

Garlic Mashed Potatoes

152

Green Beans with Mushroom Butter

147

Apple Tarts

176

SERVES 2

DRY BLACKTHORN
ENGLISH FERMENTED
CIDER *OR*
MERIDIAN EDNA VALLEY
CHARDONNAY 1990

Pasta with Bell Peppers, Goat Cheese, and Basil

SUMMER HARVEST LUNCHEON

Bruschetta with Tomato, Anchovy, and Garlic

42

Pasta with Bell Peppers, Goat Cheese, and Basil

165

Mixed Greens Salad

Zabaglione Mousse

184

SERVES 2

DOLCETTO D'ALBA
1990,
CANTINA VIETTI

Open-Faced Fried Shrimp Sandwiches with Ginger Mayonnaise

LUNCH
BEFORE THE GAME

Carrot Soup with Dill and Sour Cream

59

*Open-Faced Fried Shrimp Sandwiches
with Ginger Mayonnaise*

85

Mixed Greens Salad or Sliced Tomatoes

Chocolate Apricot Bread Pudding

185

SERVES 2

ROLLING ROCK
EXTRA PALE
PREMIUM BEER

Grilled Skirt Steak with Parsley Jalapeño Sauce; Brown Buttered Corn with Basil

DINNER ON THE PATIO

Lobster-Salad-Stuffed Eggs

38

Grilled Skirt Steak with Parsley Jalapeño Sauce

92

Brown Buttered Corn with Basil

150

Sliced Tomatoes

Warm Upside-Down Cheesecakes with Blueberry Sauce

172

SERVES 2

GUNDLACH-BUNDSCHU
SONOMA VALLEY
CABERNET-SAUVIGNON
1988

Ginger Poached Apricot and Raspberry Compote

AN ELEGANT
SPRING DINNER

Leek, Green Pea, and Potato Soup

60

Rack of Lamb with Tarragon Lemon Sauce

99

Herbed New Potatoes

152

Honey-Glazed Baby Carrots

149

Gingered Poached Apricot and Raspberry Compote

177

SERVES 2

CHATEAU
CHASSE-SPLEEN,
MOULIS-EN-MEDOC,
1985

Teriyaki-Style Chicken; Snow Pea and Green Bean Salad

A CASUAL
SUMMER DINNER

Coriander Peanut Sauce with Crudités

45

Teriyaki-Style Chicken

110

Snow Pea and Green Bean Salad

164

Spicy Rice Pilaf

142

Nectarine Crisp

180

SERVES 2

GREENWOOD RIDGE
ANDERSON VALLEY
WHITE RIESLING 1991

Poached Scrod with Herbs and Warm Vinaigrette; Vegetable Ribbons with Horseradish Lemon Butter

DINNER FOR
A SPECIAL OCCASION

Goat Cheese, Bacon, and Pine Nut Bites

43

Poached Scrod with Herbs and Warm Vinaigrette

72

Vegetable Ribbons with Horseradish Lemon Butter

155

Crisp Shallot Rice

142

Chocolate Sponge Moons Filled with Peaches and Cream

179

SERVES 2

KUNDE
SONOMA VALLEY
SAUVIGNON BLANC
1991

the recipes

Bruschetta with Tomato, Anchovy, and Garlic

F rom substantial first courses, to informal hors d'oeuvres, to light dips and spreads, our starters set the stage for any great meal to come. You can choose Mushrooms with Chicken Liver Filling or Lobster-Salad-Stuffed Eggs when the tone is elegant. Or, to begin a casual evening, maybe Bruschetta with Tomato, Anchovy, and Garlic, or Raisin Pecan Spread with toasts will do the trick.

But don't think of these recipes as *just* starters. While all are a perfect way to begin a meal, they're also terrific on their own—some as light entrées and others as quick snacks. For example, our impressive first course of Corn and Zucchini Dumplings with Jalapeño Vinegar can also double as a satisfying luncheon entrée. Or perhaps our refreshing Fruit-Stuffed Avocado bursting with banana, pineapple, and orange will be all you need for supper on a hot summer evening. When you are looking for delicious "finger food" to have with a cocktail, or to snack on while you put the finishing touches on the meal, turn to our hors d'oeuvres, spreads, and dips. These pre-dinner bites can be enjoyed anytime and make great treats. Spicy Cheddar Puffs, Baked Spinach Balls with Yogurt Dill Dip, and Herbed Ricotta Spread with crudités are just a few of the temptations that await.

First Courses
❦ ❦ ❦

Fruit-Stuffed Avocado

⅓ cup sliced banana
⅓ cup fresh or canned unsweetened pineapple
    chunks
⅓ navel orange, peel and pith discarded, cut
    into chunks
1 tablespoon vegetable oil
1 tablespoon distilled white vinegar
1 avocado, halved, peeled if desired, pitted,
    and rubbed with lemon juice
chopped dry-roasted unsalted peanuts for
    garnish

In a bowl combine the banana, the pineapple, and the orange. In a small bowl whisk the oil with the vinegar until the mixture is emulsified, add the dressing to the fruit, and toss the mixture. Spoon the fruit into the avocado halves and sprinkle it with the peanuts. Serves 2 as a first course or light entrée.

Coriander Gazpacho-Filled Avocado

1½ tablespoons finely chopped scallion
¼ cup seeded and finely chopped tomato
3 tablespoons peeled, seeded, and finely
    chopped cucumber
2 tablespoons finely chopped fresh coriander
½ teaspoon minced drained bottled pickled
    jalapeño chili (wear rubber gloves), or
    to taste
1 small garlic clove, minced
1½ to 2 teaspoons fresh lemon juice,
    or to taste, plus additional for brushing
    the avocado
1 avocado (preferably California)
corn tortilla chips as an accompaniment

In a small bowl combine the scallion, the tomato, the cucumber, the coriander, the *jalapeño*, the garlic, the lemon juice, and salt to taste. Halve and pit the avocado. Scoop out enough of the avocado flesh to leave a ¼-inch shell and chop the flesh coarse. Add the chopped avocado to the bowl, stirring gently to just combine the ingredients. Brush the avocado halves with the additional lemon juice, divide the filling between them, and serve the avocado with the tortilla chips. Serves 2.

Lobster-Salad-Stuffed Eggs

¼ pound cooked lobster meat or the meat of
    1 cooked King crab leg, chopped fine (about
    ½ cup)
2 radishes, chopped fine
2 tablespoons finely chopped scallion
2 tablespoons finely chopped celery
1 tablespoon minced fresh parsley leaves
2 tablespoons mayonnaise
2 teaspoons fresh lemon juice
⅛ teaspoon Tabasco
3 hard-boiled large eggs
½ cup finely shredded romaine for garnish
½ cup finely shredded cabbage for garnish

In a bowl combine well the lobster meat, the radishes, the scallion, the celery, the parsley, the mayonnaise, the lemon juice, the Tabasco, and salt and pepper to taste. Halve the eggs crosswise and remove the yolks. Chop 1 of the yolks, reserving the other 2 for another use, and stir it into the lobster salad. Divide the romaine and the cabbage between 2 salad plates, forming nests, fill the egg whites with the lobster salad, and arrange the eggs in the nests. Serves 2.

Photo on page 39

Lobster-Salad-Stuffed Eggs

Whole Baked Garlic and Goat Cheese with Toasts

1 large head of garlic
3 tablespoons olive oil
ten ⅓-inch-thick diagonal slices of Italian or French bread
3½ ounces (½ cup) mild goat cheese such as Montrachet, softened

Cut off the top quarter of the head of garlic with a sharp knife to expose the cloves, set the garlic in the middle of a large piece of foil, and drizzle it with 2 teaspoons of the oil. Crimp the foil around the garlic to enclose it completely and bake the garlic in the middle of a preheated 425° F. oven for 40 minutes. While the garlic is baking, brush the bread slices with the remaining oil and bake them on a baking sheet in the lower third of the oven (below the garlic), turning them once, for 10 to 12 minutes, or until they are golden and crisp. Unwrap the garlic and put it and the goat cheese on a serving plate surrounded by the toasts. To serve the garlic: Remove the softened cloves with a knife or fork, or turn the head of garlic upside down and squeeze out the cloves. Spread the garlic, the cheese, and salt and pepper to taste on the toasts. Serves 2.

Corn and Zucchini Dumplings with Jalapeño Vinegar

For the jalapeño **vinegar**
2 tablespoons white-wine vinegar
1 teaspoon minced drained bottled pickled
   jalapeño chili (wear rubber gloves)
¼ teaspoon sugar, or to taste
1 tablespoon minced fresh basil leaves

For the filling
¼ cup cooked fresh corn or thawed frozen
¼ cup finely chopped seeded tomato
¼ cup finely chopped zucchini
2 tablespoons cream cheese, softened
2 tablespoons minced fresh basil leaves

12 won ton wrappers (available at Asian
   markets and many supermarkets),
   thawed if frozen, covered with a
   dampened kitchen towel
1 tablespoon vegetable oil
½ cup water

Make the *jalapeño* vinegar: In a small bowl combine well the vinegar, the *jalapeño*, the sugar, the basil, and salt to taste.

Make the filling: In a bowl combine well the corn, the tomato, the zucchini, the cream cheese, the basil, and salt to taste.

Put 1 won ton wrapper on a work surface, moisten the edges lightly with water, and mound 2 level teaspoons of the filling in the center. Fold the wrapper over the filling to form a triangle, pressing out the air and pinching the edges firmly to seal them well, and cover the dumpling with a dampened kitchen towel. Make dumplings with the remaining wrappers and filling in the same manner, covering them as they are made.

In a non-stick skillet large enough to hold the dumplings in one layer heat the oil over high heat until it is hot but not smoking, arrange the dumplings in the skillet so that each stands upright on its folded edge, and cook them over moderately high heat, shaking the skillet occasionally, for 2 minutes, or until the undersides are golden brown and crisped. Add the water to the skillet and steam the dumplings, covered, over moderately low heat for 5 minutes. Remove the lid and continue to cook the dumplings over moderately high heat until all of the liquid is evaporated and the undersides are recrisped. Transfer the dumplings to a heated platter and pour the *jalapeño* vinegar over them. Serves 2 as a first course or luncheon entrée.

Sausage and Bell Pepper Hush Puppies with Mustard Sauce

For the mustard sauce
¼ cup sour cream
1 tablespoon Dijon-style mustard
fresh lemon juice to taste

¼ pound *kielbasa* **or other cooked smoked**
   sausage, quartered lengthwise and cut
   crosswise into ¼-inch pieces
½ cup chopped red bell pepper
½ teaspoon vegetable oil plus additional for
   deep-frying the hush puppies
1 large egg
¼ cup milk
½ cup yellow cornmeal
¼ cup all-purpose flour
1¼ teaspoons double-acting baking powder
⅛ teaspoon cayenne, or to taste

¼ teaspoon salt
¼ cup thinly sliced scallion

Make the mustard sauce: In a small bowl whisk together the sour cream, the mustard, the lemon juice, and salt to taste.

In a skillet cook the *kielbasa* and the bell pepper in ½ teaspoon of the oil over moderate heat, stirring occasionally, for 5 minutes, or until the bell pepper is crisp-tender. In a bowl whisk together the egg and the milk, into the bowl sift together the cornmeal, the flour, the baking powder, the cayenne, and the salt, and whisk the mixture until it is combined well.

Transfer the *kielbasa* mixture with a slotted spoon to the bowl, add the scallion, and stir the batter until it is just combined. In a deep skillet or deep fryer heat 1½ inches of the additional oil to 320° F., add tablespoons of the batter, and fry the hush puppies, turning them once, for 1½ to 2 minutes, or until they are golden, transferring them with a slotted spoon as they are fried to paper towels to drain. Serve the hush puppies with the mustard sauce. Makes about 10 hush puppies.

Photo on this page

Sausage and Bell Pepper Hush Puppies with Mustard Sauce

Mushrooms with Chicken Liver Filling

**6 large mushrooms, stems removed and
minced**
2 tablespoons minced onion
1 tablespoon plus 1 teaspoon unsalted butter
2 tablespoons vegetable oil
**¼ pound chicken livers, rinsed, trimmed,
patted dry, and chopped**
2 tablespoons medium-dry Sherry
1 tablespoon minced fresh parsley leaves
1 tablespoon finely sliced scallion greens
¼ cup fine fresh bread crumbs
1½ teaspoons Dijon-style mustard
2 tablespoons freshly grated Parmesan

In a small skillet cook the mushroom stems
and the onion in 1 tablespoon of the butter
and 1 tablespoon of the oil over moderate
heat, stirring, for 5 minutes, add the livers,
and cook the mixture, stirring, until the livers
are browned on the outside but still pink within. Stir in the Sherry, the parsley, and the scallion greens, bring the mixture to a boil, and
remove the skillet from the heat. Season the
mixture with salt and pepper and toss it with
2 tablespoons of the bread crumbs.

Brush the inside of the mushroom caps
with the mustard, in a small skillet brown the
mushrooms rounded side down in the remaining 1 tablespoon oil over moderate heat for
2 minutes, or until they are heated through,
and transfer them to a shallow baking dish.
Divide the liver mixture among the caps,
mounding it. Toss the Parmesan with the
remaining 2 tablespoons bread crumbs, sprinkle
the mixture over the mushroom caps, patting it
down, and dot the mushrooms with the
remaining 1 teaspoon butter. Bake the mushrooms in a preheated 400° F. oven for 15 minutes. Serves 2.

42

Hors d'Oeuvres

Artichoke Heart and Sun-Dried Tomato Canapés

¼ cup minced onion
2 teaspoons olive oil
1 tablespoon minced fresh parsley leaves
**2 tablespoons minced drained sun-dried
tomatoes**
**4½ ounces frozen artichoke hearts, cooked
according to the package instructions,
drained, and chopped (about ¾ cup)**
¼ cup sour cream
**3 slices of homemade-type white bread,
crusts discarded, toasted lightly, and halved
diagonally**

In a small skillet cook the onion in the olive
oil over moderately low heat, stirring occasionally, until it is softened and stir in the parsley,
the sun-dried tomatoes, the artichokes, the
sour cream, and salt and pepper to taste.
Divide the mixture among the toasts, mounding it, and broil the toasts on the rack of a
broiler pan about 4 inches from the heat until
they are browned lightly. Makes 6 canapés,
serving 2.

Bruschetta with Tomato, Anchovy, and Garlic

eight ⅓-inch-thick slices of Italian bread
**2 tablespoons olive oil (preferably
extra-virgin)**
1 garlic clove, halved
**3 plum tomatoes, seeded and chopped
into ¼-inch pieces (½ cup)**
1 anchovy fillet, minced
1 tablespoon minced fresh basil leaves
**½ teaspoon balsamic vinegar (available at
specialty foods shops and some markets)**
¼ teaspoon sugar

Toast the bread slices on a baking sheet in the upper third of a preheated 500° F. oven for 4 minutes, or until they are golden. While the toasts are warm, brush both sides of the toasts with the oil and rub them with the garlic. In a bowl combine the tomatoes, the anchovy, the basil, the balsamic vinegar, the sugar, and salt and pepper to taste and top the toasts with the mixture. Makes 8 hors d'oeuvres, serving 2.

Photo on page 36

Spicy Cheddar Puffs

¼ cup milk
¼ cup water
½ stick (¼ cup) unsalted butter
¼ teaspoon salt
⅛ teaspoon cayenne
½ cup all-purpose flour
2 large eggs
1 cup grated extra-sharp Cheddar

In a small heavy saucepan combine the milk, the water, the butter, the salt, and the cayenne and bring the mixture to a boil over high heat. Reduce the heat to moderate, add the flour all at once, and beat the mixture with a wooden spoon until it leaves the side of the pan. Beat the mixture for 1 minute. Transfer the mixture to a bowl, whisk in the eggs, 1 at a time, whisking well after each addition, and stir in the Cheddar. Drop the batter in 8 mounds on a buttered baking sheet and bake the puffs in the upper third of a preheated 400° F. oven for 20 minutes, or until they are crisp and golden. The puffs may be served as an hors d'oeuvre or as an accompaniment to soups, meats, and poultry. *The puffs may be made 1 day in advance, kept in an airtight container, and reheated in a 400° F. oven for 5 minutes.* Makes 8 puffs.

Goat Cheese, Bacon, and Pine Nut Bites

¼ cup (about 2 ounces) mild goat cheese
1 slice of bacon, cooked until crisp, drained, cooled, and chopped fine
1 tablespoon minced scallion greens
½ cup pine nuts, toasted lightly and cooled

In a bowl mash together the goat cheese, the bacon, and the scallion greens. Form level teaspoons of the mixture into balls. (If the mixture is too soft to form, chill it for 10 minutes.) Coat the balls with the pine nuts, pressing the nuts into the mixture, and chill them for 20 minutes. Makes about 12 bites, serving 2.

Mushroom Pâté

1 slice of whole-wheat bread
⅓ cup heavy cream
½ pound mushrooms, chopped fine
¼ cup minced onion
2 tablespoons unsalted butter
1 tablespoon minced fresh parsley leaves
a pinch of dried orégano, crumbled
a pinch of dried basil, crumbled
2 ounces cream cheese, softened
1 tablespoon Cognac
French bread slices as an accompaniment

In a small bowl let the whole-wheat bread soak in the cream. In a skillet sauté the mushrooms and the onion in the butter over moderately high heat, stirring occasionally, for 3 to 4 minutes, or until the liquid is evaporated and the vegetables are softened. Transfer the mixture to a bowl, add the parsley, and let the mixture cool, stirring occasionally. Blend in the bread mixture, the orégano, the basil, the cream cheese, the Cognac, and salt and pepper to taste. Transfer the pâté to a serving bowl and chill it for 20 minutes. Serve the pâté with the French bread. Serves 2.

43

Hot Spiced Pecans

**2 tablespoons chopped onion, pressed
    through a garlic press, reserving the juice
    and the pulp**
1½ teaspoons soy sauce
2 tablespoons unsalted butter, melted
½ teaspoon salt
¼ teaspoon cayenne
1 cup pecan halves

In a bowl combine the onion juice and pulp,
the soy sauce, the butter, the salt, and the
cayenne and add the pecans, stirring them to
coat them with the mixture. Bake the pecans
on a jelly-roll pan in a preheated 300° F. oven,
stirring occasionally, for 25 minutes. Transfer
the pecans to paper towels to drain and let
them cool. Serves 2.

Baked Spinach Balls with Yogurt Dill Dip

1 cup water
a 10-ounce package frozen leaf spinach
¼ cup minced shallot
½ cup fine fresh bread crumbs
1 large egg, beaten lightly
¼ cup freshly grated Parmesan
2 teaspoons fresh lemon juice

For the yogurt dill dip
¼ cup plain yogurt
2 teaspoons minced fresh dill
**1 small garlic clove, minced and mashed to a
    paste with ¼ teaspoon salt**

In a saucepan bring the water to a boil, add
the spinach, and cook it for 3 minutes, or
until it is just tender. Drain the spinach, let it
cool, and squeeze it dry by the handful. Chop
the spinach fine and in a bowl combine it well
with the shallot, the bread crumbs, the egg,
the Parmesan, the lemon juice, and salt and
pepper to taste. Roll the spinach mixture into
twenty 1-inch balls and bake the spinach balls
on a baking sheet in the middle of a preheated
400° F. oven for 12 minutes, or until they just
begin to turn golden.

Make the yogurt dill dip: In a small bowl
stir together the yogurt, the dill, and the garlic
paste and serve the baked spinach balls with
the dip. Makes 20 spinach balls.

Spreads and Dips

Raisin Pecan Spread

½ cup raisins
5 tablespoons fresh orange juice
¼ cup pecans, toasted lightly
**buttered thin toast or apple slices as an
    accompaniment**

In a saucepan simmer the raisins with 4 tablespoons of the orange juice over moderate heat,
stirring occasionally, until the liquid is reduced
to about 1 tablespoon. In a food processor
purée the raisin mixture with the pecans,
blending in the remaining 1 tablespoon orange
juice if desired, and serve the spread on the
toast. Makes about ⅓ cup, serving 2.

Herbed Ricotta Spread

15 ounces whole-milk ricotta
2 tablespoons minced scallion
2½ tablespoons minced fresh parsley leaves
2 tablespoons minced radish
¼ teaspoon minced garlic
¼ cup fresh lemon juice, or to taste
2 tablespoons plain yogurt
cayenne to taste
***crudités* as an accompaniment**

In a ceramic or glass bowl combine the ricotta, the scallion, the parsley, the radish, the garlic, the lemon juice, the yogurt, the cayenne, and salt to taste. *The spread may be made 1 day in advance and kept, covered and chilled.* Serve the spread with the *crudités*. Makes about 2½ cups.

Herbed Sardine Spread

a 3¾-ounce can sardines, packed in oil,
  drained
1½ ounces cream cheese, softened
1 tablespoon minced fresh parsley leaves
1 scallion, minced
1 teaspoon fresh lemon juice, or to taste
crackers or toast points as an accompaniment

In a small bowl with a fork mash together the sardines, the cream cheese, the parsley, the scallion, the lemon juice, and pepper to taste. Serve the spread with the crackers. Makes about ½ cup, serving 2.

Chick-Pea, Cumin, and Garlic Dip

a 19-ounce can chick-peas, rinsed and
  drained well
1 small garlic clove
2 tablespoons water
3 tablespoons olive oil (preferably
  extra-virgin)
2 teaspoons fresh lemon juice, or to taste
1 teaspoon ground cumin, or to taste
assorted vegetables such as celery, carrot,
  and fennel bulb (sometimes called
  anise, available in most supermarkets),
  cut into sticks

In a food processor purée the chick-peas and the garlic with the water, the oil, the lemon juice, the cumin, and salt to taste. Transfer the dip to a bowl and serve it with the vegetables. *The spread keeps, covered and chilled, for 1 week.* Makes about 1¾ cups.

Coriander Peanut Sauce with Crudités

¼ cup smooth peanut butter
½ cup heavy cream
1 tablespoon minced fresh coriander
¼ cup minced scallion greens
1½ teaspoons fresh lemon juice, or to taste
1 small garlic clove, minced
cayenne to taste
crudités as an accompaniment

In a bowl whisk together the peanut butter, the cream, the coriander, the scallion greens, the lemon juice, the garlic, the cayenne, and salt to taste. Serve the sauce with the *crudités*. Makes about ¾ cup, serving 2.

Cucumber Spears with Smoked Salmon and Yogurt Dip

½ cup plain yogurt
2 ounces smoked salmon, chopped fine
  (about ¼ cup)
½ teaspoon drained and squeezed dry bottled
  horseradish
½ teaspoon snipped fresh dill plus 1 dill sprig
  for garnish
½ seedless cucumber, cut lengthwise into
  8 spears

Drain the yogurt in a fine sieve set over a bowl, covered and chilled, for 30 minutes. In a bowl combine the salmon, the yogurt, the horseradish, the snipped dill, and salt and pepper to taste. Transfer the sauce to a serving dish, garnish it with the dill sprig, and serve it with the cucumber spears. Serves 2.

45

Parmesan Puffs

QUICK BREADS AND PIZZAS

There is nothing more appealing and impressive than warm breads, fresh from the oven. And now, with our quick recipes, you can enjoy them even when time is tight.

Most of our biscuits, muffins, and crackers can be quickly prepared in a single bowl with double-acting baking powder and all-purpose flour. Biscuits require a simple dough that should be handled as little as possible to avoid toughening. To stamp out the biscuits you will need a 2¼-inch cutter, or, in a pinch, you can use a glass. Muffins also take only minutes to prepare. Since all our recipes make six muffins, you may want to freeze leftovers: Wrap cool muffins in foil and put them in a plastic freezer bag. To reheat them, remove them from the bag and pop them in a preheated 350° F. oven for ten minutes or until they are hot. If you like your muffins crusty, remove the foil and bake them a bit longer.

Our pizzas and flatbread can be kneaded in no time with a food processor. The fast-acting yeast they require is available in most supermarkets; it is date-coded, so be sure to check the expiration date before you buy. To retain freshness, store the yeast in the refrigerator. Keep in mind that fast-acting yeast should be mixed with *130° F.* water; a higher temperature will kill the yeast. Also note that *unbleached* all-purpose flour is used in two of our pizzas. This flour produces a stronger, more elastic dough that is ideal for pizza crust. And finally, if you prefer crisper crusts, a black steel baking sheet is best.

Quick Breads
❦ ❦ ❦

Chili Cornmeal Biscuits

⅔ cup all-purpose flour
⅓ cup plus 1 teaspoon yellow cornmeal
1½ teaspoons double-acting baking powder
¾ teaspoon chili powder
1 teaspoon sugar
½ teaspoon salt
3 tablespoons cold unsalted butter, cut
 into bits
6 tablespoons heavy cream

In a bowl stir together the flour, ⅓ cup of the cornmeal, the baking powder, the chili powder, the sugar, and the salt, add the butter, and blend the mixture until it resembles coarse meal. Add the cream and stir the mixture until it just forms a sticky dough. Gather the dough into a ball, knead it gently 6 times on a floured surface, and roll or pat it out ½ inch thick. Cut out 6 rounds with a 2¼-inch cutter dipped in flour, rerolling and cutting the scraps, and transfer them to an ungreased baking sheet. Sprinkle the remaining 1 teaspoon cornmeal over the tops of the rounds and bake the chili cornmeal biscuits in the middle of a preheated 450° F. oven for 12 to 14 minutes, or until they are golden. Makes 6 biscuits.

Parmesan Puffs

¼ cup milk
¼ cup water
½ stick (¼ cup) unsalted butter
¼ teaspoon salt
½ cup all-purpose flour
2 large eggs
1 cup freshly grated Parmesan

In a small heavy saucepan combine the milk, the water, the butter, and the salt and bring the mixture to a boil over high heat. Reduce the heat to moderate, add the flour all at once, and beat the mixture with a wooden spoon until it leaves the side of the pan and forms a ball. Transfer the mixture to a bowl, whisk in the eggs, 1 at a time, whisking well after each addition, and stir in the Parmesan and pepper to taste. Drop the batter in 8 mounds on a buttered baking sheet and bake the puffs in the upper third of a preheated 400° F. oven for 20 minutes, or until they are crisp and golden. *The puffs may be kept overnight in an airtight container.* Serve the puffs as an hors d'oeuvre or as an accompaniment to soups, meats, and poultry. Makes 8 puffs.

Photo on page 46

Mustard and Dill Biscuits

1 cup all-purpose flour
1½ teaspoons double-acting baking powder
½ teaspoon dried dillweed, crumbled
½ teaspoon salt
½ stick (¼ cup) cold unsalted butter,
 cut into bits
¼ cup milk plus additional for brushing
 the rounds
1 tablespoon coarse-grain mustard
1½ teaspoons mustard seeds

Into a bowl sift together the flour, the baking powder, the dillweed, and the salt, add the butter, and blend the mixture until it resembles coarse meal. In a small bowl combine well ¼ cup of the milk, the mustard, and the mustard seeds, add the milk mixture to the flour mixture, and stir the mixture until it just forms a sticky dough. Gather the dough into a ball, knead it gently 6 times on a floured surface, and roll or pat it out ½ inch thick. Cut out 6 rounds with a 2¼-inch round cutter dipped in flour, rerolling and cutting the scraps, and transfer them to an ungreased

baking sheet. Brush the tops of the rounds with the additional milk, bake the biscuits in the middle of a preheated 425° F. oven for 15 minutes, or until they are golden, and transfer them to a rack. Makes 6 biscuits.

Pepper Cheese Biscuits

1 cup plus 2 tablespoons all-purpose flour
1½ teaspoons double-acting baking powder
½ teaspoon salt
½ cup finely grated sharp Cheddar
2 tablespoons peeled, seeded, and chopped plum tomato
1 teaspoon minced seeded *jalapeño* chili, (wear rubber gloves)
½ cup milk

Into a bowl sift together the flour, the baking powder, and the salt, add the Cheddar, the tomato, and the *jalapeño*, and toss the mixture well. Add the milk and stir the mixture with a fork until it forms a soft, dry dough. Shape the dough into 6 balls, transfer the balls to a buttered and floured baking sheet, and pat them into 3-inch rounds. Bake the biscuits in the upper third of a preheated 450° F. oven for 15 to 18 minutes, or until they are golden brown and crusty. Serve the biscuits warm with soups or omelets. Makes 6 biscuits.

Scallion Biscuits

¾ cup all-purpose flour
1 teaspoon double-acting baking powder
¼ teaspoon baking soda
½ teaspoon salt
2 tablespoons cold unsalted butter, cut into bits
¼ cup minced scallion, including the green part
⅓ cup plain yogurt

Into a bowl sift together the flour, the baking powder, the baking soda, the salt, and freshly ground pepper to taste and blend in the butter until the mixture resembles coarse meal. Stir in the scallion and the yogurt and combine the mixture until it just forms a soft, sticky dough. Drop the dough by heaping tablespoonfuls onto a buttered baking sheet and bake the biscuits in the middle of a preheated 425° F. oven for 12 to 15 minutes, or until they are golden. Makes about 6 biscuits.

Cheddar Jalapeño Corn Bread

⅔ cup yellow cornmeal
⅓ cup all-purpose flour
1 teaspoon double-acting baking powder
½ teaspoon baking soda
½ teaspoon salt
⅔ cup coarsely grated extra-sharp Cheddar
4 tablespoons chopped drained bottled
  pimiento
1½ teaspoons finely chopped seeded bottled
  pickled *jalapeño* chili, or to taste
  (wear rubber gloves)
1 large egg
¾ cup buttermilk
½ stick (¼ cup) unsalted butter

In a bowl whisk together the cornmeal, the flour, the baking powder, the baking soda, and the salt, add the Cheddar, the pimiento, and the *jalapeño*, and toss the mixture well. In a small bowl whisk together the egg and the buttermilk. In a cast-iron or other heavy ovenproof skillet measuring 8 inches across the bottom melt the butter over moderately low heat and add half of it to the buttermilk mixture, whisking. Transfer the skillet with the remaining melted butter to the middle of a preheated 425° F. oven and heat it for 5 minutes.

While the skillet is heating, add the buttermilk mixture to the cornmeal mixture and stir the batter until it is just combined. Working quickly, remove the skillet from the oven, add the batter, smoothing the top, and bake it in the middle of the 425° F. oven for 15 to 20 minutes, or until it is golden and a tester inserted in the center comes out clean. Serve the corn bread, cut into wedges, warm or at room temperature. Serves 2 with leftovers.

Onion and Black Pepper Flatbread

1¼ cups chopped onion
2 tablespoons olive oil plus 4 teaspoons
  additional for drizzling the dough
2½ cups all-purpose flour
2½ teaspoons (a ¼-ounce package) fast-acting
  yeast (available at most supermarkets)
¾ cup hot water (130° F.)
¾ teaspoon table salt
¾ teaspoon coarsely ground pepper plus additional for sprinkling the dough
½ teaspoon coarse salt, or to taste

In a skillet cook 1 cup of the onion in 1 tablespoon of the oil over moderate heat, stirring occasionally, until it is golden. In a food processor combine 1 cup of the flour and the yeast, with the motor running add the hot water combined with 1 tablespoon of the remaining oil, and turn the motor off. Add 1¼ cups of the remaining flour, the table salt, and ¾ teaspoon of the pepper and pulse the motor 4 times. Add the cooked onion and blend the dough until it forms a ball, incorporating more of the remaining ¼ cup flour if necessary, 1 tablespoon at a time, pulsing the motor until the flour is incorporated, to keep the dough from sticking. Transfer the dough to a lightly floured surface and knead it for 15 seconds. Quarter the dough, form each piece into a ¼-inch-thick round, and put the rounds on a lightly oiled baking sheet. With a finger, press indentations firmly into the dough at 2-inch intervals, drizzle the dough with the additional 4 teaspoons oil, and sprinkle it with the remaining ¼ cup onion, the additional pepper, and the coarse salt. Bake the bread in a preheated 500° F. oven for 15 to 18 minutes, or until it is golden. *The bread may be kept, wrapped well, at room temperature for 1 day.* Makes four 5-inch breads.

QUICK BREADS AND PIZZAS

Oatmeal Raisin Yogurt Muffins

¾ cup all-purpose flour
¾ cup old-fashioned rolled oats
¼ cup sugar
1 teaspoon double-acting baking powder
½ teaspoon baking soda
½ teaspoon salt
½ teaspoon cinnamon
⅓ cup raisins
½ cup plain yogurt
¼ cup milk
½ stick (¼ cup) unsalted butter, melted and cooled
1½ teaspoons freshly grated orange zest
1 large egg, beaten lightly

In a bowl stir together the flour, the oats, the sugar, the baking powder, the baking soda, the salt, the cinnamon, and the raisins. In another bowl whisk together the yogurt, the milk, the butter, the zest, and the egg. Stir the yogurt mixture into the flour mixture and stir the batter until it is just combined. Divide the batter among 6 paper-lined ½-cup muffin tins and bake the muffins in the middle of a preheated 400° F. oven for 20 to 25 minutes, or until they are golden and a tester comes out clean. Makes 6 muffins.

Pumpkin Spice Muffins

½ cup canned pumpkin purée
½ cup firmly packed light brown sugar
¼ cup vegetable oil
1 large egg
⅔ cup all-purpose flour
¾ teaspoon double-acting baking powder
¾ teaspoon cinnamon
½ teaspoon baking soda
½ teaspoon ground ginger
¼ teaspoon ground allspice
¼ teaspoon salt
granulated sugar for sprinkling the muffins

In a bowl whisk together the pumpkin purée, the brown sugar, the oil, and the egg until the mixture is smooth. Into the bowl sift together the flour, the baking powder, the cinnamon, the baking soda, the ginger, the allspice, and the salt and stir the batter until it is combined well. Divide the batter among 6 well-buttered ½-cup muffin tins, sprinkle it with the granulated sugar, and bake the muffins in the middle of a preheated 400° F. oven for 15 to 20 minutes, or until a tester comes out clean. Turn the muffins out onto a rack and let them cool. Makes 6 muffins.

51

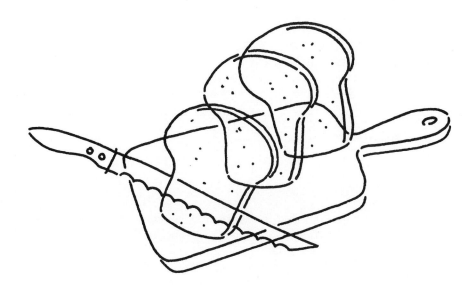

Bacon and Onion Corn Muffins

4 slices of lean bacon
3 tablespoons minced onion
½ cup yellow cornmeal
⅓ cup all-purpose flour
½ teaspoon double-acting baking powder
½ teaspoon baking soda
¼ teaspoon salt
1 large egg
2 tablespoons unsalted butter, melted
¾ cup sour cream
2 tablespoons milk

In a heavy skillet cook the bacon over moderate heat, turning it once, until it is crisp, transfer it to paper towels to drain, and crumble it. Pour off all but 1 tablespoon of the fat in the skillet and in the remaining fat cook the onion over moderately low heat, stirring occasionally, until it is softened.

Into a bowl sift together twice the cornmeal, the flour, the baking powder, the baking soda, and the salt. In another bowl whisk together the egg, the butter, the sour cream, and the milk, stir in the bacon, the onion, undrained, and the cornmeal mixture, and beat the batter well. Divide the batter among 6 well-buttered ¼-cup muffin tins and bake the muffins in a preheated 425° F. oven for 20 minutes, or until they are golden. Turn the muffins out onto a rack and serve them warm with butter. *Any leftover muffins may be kept wrapped and chilled for several days or frozen.* Makes 6 muffins.

Lemon Pepper Crackers

½ cup all-purpose flour
1 teaspoon coarsely ground black pepper
1 teaspoon freshly grated lemon zest
**2 tablespoons cold unsalted butter,
   cut into pieces**
1 tablespoon sour cream
1½ teaspoons fresh lemon juice
1 teaspoon water if necessary
coarse salt for sprinkling on the crackers

In a bowl blend the flour, the pepper, the zest, and the butter until the mixture resembles coarse meal, add the sour cream and the lemon juice, and toss the mixture, adding the water if necessary, until it just forms a dough. Gather the dough into a ball and chill it, wrapped in plastic wrap, for 15 minutes. Roll out the dough ¹⁄₁₆ inch thick on a lightly floured surface and with a 2-inch round cutter cut out 16 rounds. Bake the rounds, sprinkled with the coarse salt, on an ungreased baking sheet in the middle of a preheated 400° F. oven for 12 minutes, or until they are golden. Transfer the crackers to a rack and let them cool for 5 minutes. Makes 16 crackers.

Photo on page 62

Three-Seed Whole-Wheat Crackers

½ cup whole-wheat flour
1 tablespoon all-purpose flour
½ teaspoon double-acting baking powder
¼ teaspoon table salt
1 tablespoon cold unsalted butter
¼ cup milk
1 teaspoon sesame seeds
1 teaspoon poppy seeds
1 teaspoon caraway seeds
coarse salt to taste

Into a bowl sift together the flours, the baking powder, and the table salt and blend in the butter until the mixture resembles coarse meal. Make a well in the center, add the milk and the seeds, and combine the mixture with a fork until it just forms a soft dough. Knead the dough gently on a lightly floured surface for 30 seconds and roll it out ¹⁄₁₆ inch thick. Cut out rounds of the dough with a floured 2¼-inch cutter and transfer them to buttered baking sheets. Gather the scraps, reroll the dough, and cut out more rounds in the same manner. Prick the rounds with a fork, sprinkle them with the coarse salt, and bake them in a preheated 450° F. oven for 8 to 10 minutes, or until they are golden. *The crackers keep in an airtight container for up to 1 week.* Makes about 20 crackers.

Cumin Melba Toasts

2 tablespoons unsalted butter, melted
1 garlic clove, sliced thin lengthwise
½ teaspoon ground cumin
4 slices of homemade-style white bread

In a small saucepan melt the butter with the garlic over moderate heat, remove the pan from the heat, and let the mixture stand for 5 minutes. Stir in the cumin. Roll each slice of bread as thin as possible with a rolling pin and trim and discard the crusts. Brush both sides of the bread with the butter mixture, discarding the garlic, cut each slice diagonally into 2 triangles, and bake the triangles on a baking sheet in the middle of a preheated 350° F. oven for 7 to 8 minutes on each side, or until they are browned lightly and crisp. Cool the toasts on a rack. Serves 2.

Pizzas
❦ ❦ ❦

Zucchini and Red Bell Pepper Biscuit Pizzas

½ pound zucchini, scrubbed, quartered lengthwise, and sliced thin crosswise (about 2 cups)
1 red bell pepper, chopped
¼ cup olive oil
½ teaspoon dried orégano, crumbled
½ teaspoon dried hot red pepper flakes, or to taste
¼ cup buttermilk
1 cup all-purpose flour
1 teaspoon double-acting baking powder
¼ teaspoon baking soda
¼ teaspoon salt
½ stick (¼ cup) cold unsalted butter, cut into bits
½ to ¾ cup coarsely grated mozzarella

In a heavy skillet cook the zucchini and the bell pepper in 2 tablespoons of the oil over moderate heat, stirring occasionally, until the vegetables are crisp-tender and stir in the orégano, the red pepper flakes, and salt to taste.

In a small bowl whisk together the remaining 2 tablespoons oil and the buttermilk. In a bowl whisk together the flour, the baking powder, the baking soda, and the salt and blend in the butter until the mixture resembles coarse meal. Make a well in the center, add the buttermilk mixture, and combine the mixture with a fork until it just forms a soft dough. Knead the dough lightly on a floured surface for 30 seconds, halve it, and roll each half into an 8-inch round. Transfer the rounds carefully to a baking sheet and form a ¼-inch rim around the edge of each round. Divide the zucchini mixture between the rounds, top it with the mozzarella, and bake the pizzas in a preheated 450° F. oven for 12 to 15 minutes, or until the crusts are golden and crisp. Serves 2.

53

Individual Cornmeal Pizzette with Gorgonzola, Escarole, and Bell Pepper

Individual Mushroom, Red Onion, and Arugula Pizzas

For the crust
1½ cups unbleached all-purpose flour
1¼ teaspoons (half a ¼-ounce package)
  fast-acting yeast (available at most
  supermarkets)
½ cup hot water (130° F.)
1 tablespoon olive oil
1 teaspoon sugar
½ teaspoon salt

For the topping
2 tablespoons olive oil
¼ pound mushrooms
1 cup packed trimmed *arugula*, well rinsed
  and spun dry
½ small red onion, sliced thin lengthwise
1 large garlic clove, or to taste, minced

yellow cornmeal for sprinkling the
  baking sheet
½ cup coarsely grated mozzarella
⅓ cup freshly grated Parmesan

Make the crust: In a food processor combine ½ cup of the flour and the yeast, with the motor running add the hot water, and turn the motor off. Add the oil, the sugar, the salt, and the remaining 1 cup flour, blend the mixture until it forms a ball, and turn it out onto a lightly floured surface. Knead the dough 8 to 10 times, form it into a ball, and let it rest while making the mushroom mixture.

Make the topping: In a small heavy skillet heat the oil over moderately high heat until it is hot but not smoking and in it sauté the mushrooms, stirring occasionally, until the liquid the mushrooms give off is evaporated. Stir in the *arugula*, the onion, the garlic, and salt and pepper to taste and cook the mixture, stirring, for 2 minutes.

Halve the dough, form each half into a ball, and stretch each ball into a 7-inch round, making the rounds slightly thicker around the edges. Transfer the rounds to an oiled baking sheet (preferably black steel, for a crispier crust), sprinkled lightly with the cornmeal. Divide the topping between the rounds, sprinkle the topping with the mozzarella and the Parmesan, and bake the pizzas on the bottom rack of a preheated 500° F. oven for 10 to 12 minutes, or until the crusts are golden brown. Serves 2.

Individual Cornmeal Pizzette with Gorgonzola, Escarole, and Bell Pepper

For the dough
1 cup unbleached all-purpose flour
1¼ teaspoons (half a ¼-ounce package) fast-acting yeast (available at most supermarkets)
½ cup hot water (130° F.)
1 tablespoon olive oil
1½ teaspoons honey
½ teaspoon salt
½ cup yellow cornmeal

¼ **pound escarole, washed, spun dry, and chopped coarse (3½ cups loosely packed)**
2 **tablespoons olive oil**
1 **teaspoon minced garlic**
cornmeal for sprinkling the baking sheet
¼ **cup crumbled Gorgonzola or other blue cheese**
1 **red bell pepper, cut into julienne strips**
½ **cup finely diced whole-milk mozzarella**
1 **tablespoon minced fresh rosemary leaves or 1 teaspoon dried, crumbled**

Make the dough: In a food processor combine ½ cup of the flour and the yeast, with the motor running add the hot water, and turn the motor off. Add the oil, the honey, the salt, the cornmeal, and the remaining ½ cup flour, blend the dough until it forms a ball, and turn it out onto a lightly floured surface. Knead the dough 8 to 10 times, form it into a ball, and let it rest while making the escarole mixture.

In a heavy skillet cook the escarole in 1 tablespoon of the olive oil over moderate heat, stirring, for 1 to 2 minutes, or until it is wilted slightly, add the garlic and salt and pepper to taste, and cook the mixture, stirring, for 1 minute.

Halve the dough, form each half into a ball, and stretch each ball into a 7-inch round, making the rounds slightly thicker around the edges. Transfer the rounds to an oiled baking sheet (preferably black steel, for a crispier crust), sprinkled lightly with the cornmeal, and drizzle each round with ½ teaspoon of the remaining oil. Top the rounds evenly with the Gorgonzola, the escarole mixture, the bell pepper, and the mozzarella and sprinkle the rosemary over the topping. Drizzle the *pizzette* with the remaining 2 teaspoons olive oil and bake them on the bottom rack of a preheated 500° F. oven for 10 to 12 minutes, or until the crusts are golden and the mozzarella is bubbling. Serves 2.

Photo on page 54

Creamy Lima Bean Soup with Bacon

G one are the days when soup was strictly a remedy for colds, or when Grandma was the only one who had the time to make it. Now soup is enjoyed whenever, and as we'll show you, it need not take hours to prepare and cook.

Here are a few short cuts and pointers: Many of our soups call for chicken or beef broth. While it's always a good idea to make fresh stock when you *do* have the time (and freeze it for later use), feel free to use canned broth for these recipes. The taste will not be diminished. Some of our cold soups are milk or cream-based. These ingredients should be well-chilled beforehand to cut down on the time needed to chill the prepared soup. Most important, heat or chill your bowls (whichever is appropriate), so the soup will retain the ideal temperature. And finally, have some fun when selecting your bowls. If you're having a quick winter warm-up by the fire, for example, why not try some large cups or mugs? For an impressive soup, bring out the china!

Hot soups, cold soups, cream soups, chowders, spicy soups, vegetable soups, fruit soups—all can be found here. Be creative in using them for starters, brunches, lunches, or dinners.

Asparagus Soup with Tarragon

3 large shallots, chopped fine
1½ tablespoons unsalted butter
2 cups chicken broth
1 pound asparagus, trimmed, quartered
    lengthwise, and cut crosswise into
    ½inch pieces
½ teaspoon dried tarragon, crumbled
¼ cup plain yogurt
fresh lemon juice to taste

In a saucepan cook the shallots in the butter
over moderately low heat, stirring until they
are softened. Add the broth, the asparagus, the
tarragon, and salt and pepper to taste and simmer the mixture for 2 to 3 minutes, or until
the asparagus is crisp-tender. Transfer ¼ cup of
the asparagus with a slotted spoon to each of 2
heated soup bowls, simmer the remaining
mixture for 8 to 12 minutes more, or until the
asparagus is tender, and in a blender or food
processor purée it with the yogurt and the
lemon juice. Divide the soup between the
bowls. Makes about 2½ cups, serving 2.

Creamy Lima Bean Soup with Bacon

3 slices of lean bacon
1 small onion, chopped fine
1 cup chicken broth
1 cup water
a 10-ounce package frozen lima beans
⅓ cup thinly sliced scallion greens

In a small skillet cook the bacon over moderate heat, turning it, until it is crisp, transfer it
to paper towels to drain, and crumble it.

Transfer 1 tablespoon of the fat to a heavy
saucepan and in it cook the onion over moderately low heat, stirring, until it is softened.
Add the broth, the water, and the lima beans,
simmer the mixture for 8 minutes, or until the
beans are tender, and season it with the salt
and pepper to taste. In a blender or food
processor, purée the soup, return it to the pan,
and heat it over moderate heat until it is hot.
Ladle the soup into 2 heated bowls and sprinkle it with the scallion greens and the bacon.
Makes about 3 cups, serving 2.

Photo on page 56

Brussels Sprouts Soup

10 ounces fresh Brussels sprouts, trimmed,
    or a 10-ounce package frozen Brussels
    sprouts, thawed
½ pound *kielbasa* or other smoked sausage,
    sliced ¼ inch thick
6 tablespoons minced onion
2 small boiling potatoes, cut into ½-inch cubes
2 cups chicken broth
1 cup water

Reserve ½ cup of the smallest Brussels sprouts
and in a food processor chop coarse the
remaining Brussels sprouts. In a large saucepan
brown the sausage over moderately high heat,
turning it, and drain it on paper towels. In the
fat remaining in the saucepan cook the onion
over moderately low heat, stirring, until it is
softened and add the chopped Brussels
sprouts, the whole Brussels sprouts, the
sausage, the potatoes, the broth, and the water.
Bring the liquid to a boil and simmer the soup
for 15 to 20 minutes, or until the vegetables
are tender. Divide the soup between 2 heated
bowls. Makes 4 cups, serving 2.

White Bean Soup with Prosciutto and Sage

2 ounces prosciutto, cut into ¼-inch pieces
1 tablespoon olive oil
1 onion, finely chopped
1 teaspoon minced garlic
1 bay leaf
½ teaspoon dried sage, crumbled
a 19-ounce can white beans, rinsed in a
   colander and drained well
1½ cups chicken broth
¼ cup dry white wine or dry vermouth
1 teaspoon red-wine vinegar, or to taste

In a heavy saucepan cook the prosciutto over moderately low heat, stirring occasionally, for 1 minute, add the oil and the onion, and cook the mixture over moderately low heat, stirring, until the onion is softened. Add the garlic, the bay leaf, and the sage and cook the mixture, covered, over moderate heat, stirring occasionally, for 5 minutes. In a blender or food processor purée 1 cup of the beans with ½ cup of the broth and add the purée to the vegetable mixture with the remaining 1 cup broth, the wine, and salt and pepper to taste. Simmer the mixture, covered, for 10 minutes, stir in the remaining beans, the vinegar, and salt and pepper to taste, and simmer the soup, covered, stirring occasionally, for 10 minutes. Discard the bay leaf and divide the soup between 2 heated bowls. Makes about 3 cups, serving 2.

Carrot Soup with Dill and Sour Cream

59

¼ cup finely chopped onion
1 tablespoon unsalted butter
1½ cups finely chopped peeled carrot (about
   3 carrots)
1¾ cups chicken broth
1 tablespoon minced fresh dill
⅓ cup sour cream
1 teaspoon fresh lemon juice

In a heavy saucepan cook the onion in the butter over moderately low heat, stirring, until it is softened. Add the carrots, the broth, and black pepper to taste and simmer the mixture for 13 to 15 minutes, or until the carrots are tender. Purée the mixture in a blender or food processor with the dill, transfer the purée to a saucepan, and whisk in the sour cream, the lemon juice, and salt to taste. Heat the soup over moderately low heat, stirring, until it is hot, but do not let it boil. Divide the soup between 2 heated bowls. Makes about 2½ cups, serving 2.

Curried Cream of Cauliflower Soup

4 cups salted water
3 cups cauliflower flowerets
⅓ cup minced onion
½ cup minced green bell pepper
½ teaspoon minced peeled fresh gingerroot
2 tablespoons unsalted butter
¼ teaspoon curry powder
½ cup heavy cream
1 tablespoon minced fresh parsley leaves
1 teaspoon snipped fresh chives if desired
cayenne to taste

In a kettle bring the salted water to a boil, in it cook the cauliflower, covered, for 5 minutes, or until it is tender, and drain it, reserving 1 cup of the cooking liquid. Chop 1 cup of the cauliflower.

In a saucepan cook the onion, the bell pepper, and the gingerroot in the butter over moderately low heat, stirring occasionally, for 3 to 5 minutes, or until the vegetables are softened, add the curry powder, and cook the vegetable mixture, stirring, for 1 minute. In a blender or food processor purée the mixture with the 2 cups unchopped cauliflower, and the 1 cup reserved cooking liquid. Transfer the purée to the saucepan, add the cream, the chopped cauliflower, the parsley, the chives if desired, the cayenne, and salt to taste, and heat the soup over moderately low heat, stirring occasionally, until it is hot. Divide the soup between 2 heated bowls. Makes about 2 cups, serving 2.

Leek, Green Pea, and Potato Soup

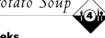

the white part of ½ pound leeks,
**   quartered lengthwise, sliced crosswise,**
**   and washed well**
a 6-ounce potato
2 tablespoons unsalted butter
2½ cups chicken broth
1 cup frozen green peas
1 tablespoon minced fresh parsley leaves plus
**   parsley leaves for garnish**
1 tablespoon chopped fresh mint leaves, or a
**   pinch of dried, crumbled**

In a large saucepan cook the leeks and the potato, peeled, quartered, and sliced thin, in the butter over moderately low heat, stirring occasionally, until the vegetables are softened and add the broth. Bring the liquid to a boil and simmer the mixture, covered, for 10 to 15 minutes, or until the potato is very soft. Stir in the peas, the parsley, and the mint, season the soup with salt and pepper to taste, and simmer it for 5 minutes. In a blender or food processor purée the soup until it is smooth and divide it between 2 heated bowls. Makes about 3 cups, serving 2.

Lentil and Vegetable Soup

1 small onion, chopped fine
1 carrot, sliced thin
1 rib of celery, sliced thin
1 tablespoon vegetable oil
1 garlic clove, minced
½ teaspoon ground cumin
¼ teaspoon ground allspice
½ cup lentils, picked over and rinsed
1¼ cups water
1¼ cups beef broth
½ cup chopped drained canned tomatoes
1 cup firmly packed coarsely chopped
**   stemmed spinach leaves, washed well**
**   and drained**
fresh lemon juice to taste

In a large heavy saucepan cook the onion, the carrot, and the celery in the oil over moderate heat, stirring, until they are lightly golden, add the garlic, the cumin, and the allspice, and cook the mixture, stirring, for 30 seconds. Add the lentils and the water, bring the liquid to a boil, and simmer the mixture, covered, for 5 minutes. Add the beef broth and simmer the mixture, covered, for 25 minutes. Stir in the tomatoes and the spinach and simmer the soup, stirring occasionally, for 2 minutes. Season the soup with the lemon juice and salt and pepper to taste and divide it between 2 heated bowls. Makes about 3½ cups, serving 2.

Parsley Soup with Saffron Dumplings

2 tablespoons minced onion
1 tablespoon unsalted butter
1 cup finely chopped fresh parsley leaves
3 cups chicken broth

For the dumplings
2 tablespoons cake flour (not self-rising)
¼ teaspoon double-acting baking powder
a large pinch of saffron threads, crumbled fine
1½ teaspoons milk plus additional if necessary
2 teaspoons beaten egg

In a wide saucepan cook the minced onion in the butter over moderately low heat until it is softened, add the parsley, and cook the mixture, stirring, for 3 minutes. Stir in the broth and simmer the soup for 15 minutes.

Make the dumplings: Into a bowl sift together the flour, the baking powder, the saffron, and a pinch of salt. Make a well in the center of the mixture, add the milk and the egg, and stir the mixture, adding more milk if necessary, until it just forms a stiff dough.

Using a spoon dipped in water drop the dumplings by rounded ¼ teaspoons into the simmering soup. Let the dumplings rise to the surface, cover the pan, and simmer the

dumplings for 2 minutes on each side, or until a wooden pick comes out clean. Divide the soup between 2 heated bowls. Makes about 6 dumplings and 2½ cups soup, serving 2.

61

Red Onion Soup

1 pound (about 4) red onions, chopped
1 bay leaf
3 tablespoons unsalted butter
1½ cups dry white wine or dry vermouth
½ teaspoon sugar
2 cups beef broth
½ teaspoon Angostura bitters
freshly grated Parmesan as an accompaniment if desired

In a kettle cook the onions with the bay leaf in the butter over moderate heat, stirring occasionally, for 20 minutes, or until they are golden. Add the white wine and the sugar, bring the mixture to a boil, and boil it, stirring, for 5 minutes. Add the broth, the bitters, and salt and pepper to taste, bring the soup to a boil, and simmer it for 2 minutes. Discard the bay leaf, divide the soup between 2 heated bowls, and sprinkle it with the Parmesan. Makes about 4 cups, serving 2.

Salmon Chowder; Lemon Pepper Crackers

Orange Sweet Potato Soup

1 cup minced onion
1 carrot, sliced thin
1 bay leaf
2 tablespoons unsalted butter
1 large sweet potato (¾ pound), peeled,
  quartered lengthwise, and sliced thin

1 small boiling potato (¼ pound), peeled,
  halved lengthwise, and sliced thin
2 cups chicken broth plus additional for
  thinning the soup
1 teaspoon freshly grated orange zest
½ cup water
⅓ cup freshly squeezed orange juice
plain yogurt as an accompaniment

In a large saucepan cook the onion, the carrot, and the bay leaf in the butter over moderately low heat, stirring occasionally, for 5 to 6 minutes, or until the onion is softened. Add the sweet potato, the boiling potato, 2 cups of the broth, the orange zest, and the water and bring the liquid to a boil. Simmer the mixture, covered, for 20 to 25 minutes, or until the potatoes are very soft, and discard the bay leaf. In a blender or food processor purée the mixture with the orange juice in batches, transferring it as it is puréed to a saucepan. Thin the mixture with the additional broth to the desired consistency and season the soup with salt and pepper. Heat the soup over moderately high heat, stirring, until it is heated through, ladle it into 2 heated bowls, and top each serving with a dollop of the yogurt. Makes about 4 cups, serving 2.

Salmon Chowder

½ pound boiling potatoes
½ teaspoon salt
2½ cups milk
¾ cup minced onion
2 tablespoons unsalted butter
½ pound salmon steak, skinned and boned
white pepper to taste
1 tablespoon fresh lemon juice
1 tablespoon all-purpose flour
2 ounces smoked salmon, chopped fine, if desired
2 tablespoons snipped fresh dill or 2 teaspoons dried, crumbled
lemon pepper crackers (page 52) as an accompaniment

In a saucepan combine the potatoes, peeled and cut into ¼-inch cubes, ¼ teaspoon of the salt, and the milk, bring the liquid to a boil, and simmer the potatoes for 10 minutes, or until they are almost tender. In another saucepan cook the onion in the butter over moderately low heat, stirring occasionally, until it is softened, put the salmon steak on the onion, and sprinkle it with the remaining ¼ teaspoon salt, the white pepper, and the lemon juice. Cook the salmon, its surface covered with a buttered round of wax paper and the pan covered with a lid, turning it once, for 8 to 10 minutes, or until it is just firm to the touch, and transfer the salmon with a slotted spatula to a plate. Sprinkle the flour over the onion and cook the mixture, stirring, for 3 minutes. Add the milk mixture, whisking, and simmer the mixture, stirring occasionally, for 5 minutes. Add the salmon steak, breaking it into chunks, the smoked salmon, the dill, and additional white pepper and salt to taste and cook the chowder over moderate heat, stirring occasionally, until it is heated through. Ladle the chowder into 2 heated bowls and serve it with the lemon pepper crackers. Makes about 4 cups, serving 2.

Photo on page 62

63

Butternut Squash and Apple Soup

1 small onion, chopped fine
1 small rib of celery, chopped fine
1 carrot, chopped fine
1 tablespoon unsalted butter
1 small butternut squash, halved lengthwise, seeded, strings discarded, cut into slices, peeled, and chopped
1 small tart green apple, peeled and cut into ½-inch cubes
2 cups chicken broth
a pinch of freshly grated nutmeg, or to taste

In a saucepan cook the onion, the celery, and the carrot in the butter over moderately low heat, stirring occasionally, for 3 minutes. Add the squash, the apple, and the broth, bring the liquid to a boil over moderately high heat, and simmer the mixture, covered, for 10 to 12 minutes, or until the squash is tender. In a blender or food processor purée the mixture, transfer the soup to the pan, and add the nutmeg and salt and pepper to taste. Heat the soup over moderate heat until it is hot and ladle it into 2 heated bowls. Makes about 2½ cups, serving 2.

Mexican Tomato Soup with Coriander and Lime

2½ cups chicken broth
1 cup tomato juice
⅓ cup water
1 small clove garlic, minced
2 tablespoons minced fresh coriander
1 tablespoon fresh lime juice

In a saucepan combine the chicken broth, the tomato juice, the water, and the garlic, bring the liquid to a boil, and simmer the mixture for 10 minutes. Stir in the coriander, the lime juice, and salt and pepper to taste, simmer the broth for 3 minutes, and ladle it into 2 heated bowls. Makes about 3¾ cups, serving 2.

Vegetable and Bacon Chowder

4 slices of lean bacon, chopped coarse
½ cup chopped onion
⅓ cup finely chopped red bell pepper
1 small yellow summer squash, halved lengthwise and cut into ¼-inch slices
½ pound small red potatoes, unpeeled and cut into ¼-inch pieces
2 cups milk
½ cup heavy cream
½ teaspoon Worcestershire sauce
1 to 2 teaspoons minced fresh dill, or to taste

In a saucepan cook the bacon over moderate heat, stirring occasionally, until it is crisp and transfer it with a slotted spoon to paper towels to drain. Discard all but 1 tablespoon of the bacon fat and in the fat remaining in the pan cook the onion and the bell pepper over moderately low heat, stirring occasionally, until the vegetables are softened. Stir in the squash, the red potatoes, the milk, the heavy cream, the Worcestershire sauce, and the dill and simmer the mixture, stirring occasionally, for 20 minutes, or until the potatoes are tender. Season the chowder with salt and pepper, divide it between 2 heated bowls, and sprinkle it with the bacon. Makes about 3½ cups, serving 2.

Scandinavian Vegetable Soup with Shrimp

1 carrot, sliced thin
⅓ cup shelled fresh peas or frozen peas, thawed
1 cup ½-inch cauliflower flowerets
1 small boiling potato, peeled, cut into ¼-inch dice, and reserved in a bowl of water
¼ pound green beans, trimmed and cut into ½-inch pieces
2 cups cold salted water
2 ounces fresh spinach, coarse stems discarded and the leaves washed well, spun dry, and chopped fine (about 1 cup)

½ cup half-and-half
1 large egg yolk
¼ pound small shrimp, shelled, deveined
  if desired
1 teaspoon salt
1 tablespoon finely chopped fresh dill
  plus 2 dill sprigs for garnish
1 teaspoon dry Sherry if desired

In a large saucepan combine the carrot, the peas, the cauliflower, the potato, drained, and the green beans with the water and boil the mixture for 7 minutes, or until the vegetables are tender. Add the spinach and cook the mixture, stirring, for 1 minute. In a small bowl whisk together the half-and-half and the yolk, stir in 1 cup of the vegetable mixture, a little at a time, and stir the yolk mixture gradually back into the pan. Cook the mixture, stirring, for 1 minute, or until a thermometer registers 160° F. (but do not let it boil). Add the shrimp and simmer the mixture for 1 minute, or until the shrimp are pink and just firm. Add the salt, the chopped dill, pepper to taste, and the Sherry, divide the soup between 2 large heated soup bowls, and garnish each serving with a dill sprig. Serves 2.

Photo on page 14

Cold Soups

Chilled Blueberry Soup

1½ cups well-chilled fresh blueberries, rinsed
  and picked over, or 12 ounces frozen
  blueberries, thawed and drained
½ cup well-chilled green grapes
½ cup well-chilled sour cream
2 teaspoons fresh lemon juice
¼ teaspoon sugar, or to taste
½ cup well-chilled seltzer or club soda

In a blender or food processor purée the blueberries and the grapes and strain the mixture through a sieve into a bowl, pushing hard on the solids. Whisk in the sour cream, the lemon juice, and the sugar, stir in the seltzer, and serve the blueberry soup immediately in 2 chilled bowls. Makes about 1¾ cups, serving 2.

Chilled Cream of Lemon Soup

⅓ cup fresh lemon juice
two 1½-inch strips of lemon zest
3 cups chicken broth
1½ tablespoons cornstarch dissolved in
  2 tablespoons chicken broth or water
½ cup well-chilled heavy cream
snipped fresh chives for garnish

In a saucepan combine the lemon juice, the lemon zest, and the chicken broth, bring the liquid to a boil, and boil it for 5 minutes. Discard the zest, stir the cornstarch mixture, and whisk it into the broth mixture. Cook the broth over moderately high heat, stirring, until it is thickened, remove the pan from the heat, and stir in the cream. In a blender or a food processor blend the soup with ½ cup crushed ice until it is smooth and transfer it to a metal bowl. Skim the froth and chill the soup, covered and set in a bowl of crushed ice and ice water, stirring occasionally, for 30 minutes. Season the soup with salt, ladle it into 2 chilled bowls, and garnish it with the chives. Makes about 3 cups, serving 2.

Chilled Senegalese Soup with Coriander

2 cups chicken broth
½ skinless boneless chicken breast (about 5 ounces)
1 onion, chopped
¾ cup chopped celery
2 tablespoons vegetable oil
1 tablespoon curry powder

1 teaspoon turmeric
a pinch of cayenne, or to taste
2 tablespoons bottled mango chutney
2 tablespoons minced fresh coriander plus, if desired, 2 sprigs for garnish

In a small saucepan bring the chicken broth to a boil and in it poach the chicken at a bare simmer, covered, for 8 minutes, or until it is springy to the touch and just cooked through. While the chicken is poaching, in a saucepan

Chilled Senegalese Soup with Coriander

cook the onion and the celery in the oil over moderately low heat, stirring occasionally, until the vegetables are softened, stir in the curry powder, the turmeric, and the cayenne, and cook the mixture, stirring, for 2 minutes. Transfer the chicken to a work surface, reserving the broth, and chop it. Add the reserved broth to the vegetable mixture, bring the mixture to a boil, stirring, and simmer it for 5 minutes. In a blender or food processor purée the mixture with the chutney and half the chicken until the purée is very smooth and transfer the purée to a metal bowl set in a larger bowl of ice and cold water. Stir the purée until it is cold, stir in the remaining chicken and the minced coriander, and divide the soup between 2 chilled bowls. Garnish each serving with a coriander sprig. Makes about 3 cups, serving 2.

Photo on page 66

Chilled Cream of Cucumber Soup with Dill

2 cucumbers, peeled and seeded
½ cup chilled buttermilk
½ cup chilled sour cream
2½ teaspoons distilled white vinegar
1 teaspoon olive oil
1½ teaspoons snipped fresh dill or
½ teaspoon dried, crumbled

In a blender or food processor purée coarse the cucumbers. In a metal bowl whisk the cucumbers with the buttermilk, the sour cream, the vinegar, the oil, the dill, and salt to taste and chill the soup, covered and set in a bowl of crushed ice and ice water, stirring occasionally, for 30 minutes. Divide the soup between 2 chilled bowls. Makes about 2 cups, serving 2.

Cold Spicy Tomato Soup with Avocado and Chives

1½ pounds tomatoes, peeled, seeded,
and chopped
½ cup well-chilled beef broth
½ teaspoon Tabasco, or to taste
½ California avocado, cut into ½-inch dice
2 teaspoons minced fresh chives

In a blender or food processor purée the chopped tomatoes. In a metal bowl whisk together the purée, the broth, the Tabasco, and salt and pepper to taste, set the bowl in a bowl of ice and cold water, and stir the soup until it is cold. Divide the avocado and the chives between 2 chilled bowls and ladle the soup over them. Makes about 3 cups, serving 2.

Marinated Salmon Seared in a Pepper Crust; Creamed Corn and Red Bell Pepper; Tomato, Cucumber, and Feta Salad

FISH

L ow in saturated fats and cholesterol, high in vitamins and minerals, fish is one of the most healthful foods you can eat. *And*, when it is combined with a simple sauce, it is one of the most elegant and easy dishes to serve. All of our fish recipes call for fillets or steaks, both cuts that require minimal cooking time.

Buy only the freshest fish. The flesh of the fillets and steaks should be translucent, firm, and without traces of blood or bruises of any kind. Never buy or eat fish that smells fishy. And, for health reasons, make sure that your utensils and boards are squeaky-clean.

When using fillets, you will need to check for bones by running your finger near the wide (head) end of the fish and down the center. Take tweezers and pluck out any bones by pulling toward the wide end of the fillet.

If you need to remove the skin from a fillet, place the fillet on a board with the tail end facing you and pin down the tail end with the fingertips of one hand. With an 8- or 10-inch chef's knife in the other hand, place the blade at an angle in front of your fingertips and between the fillet and the skin. Gently saw back and forth, separating the flesh from the skin, and proceed up the fillet, lifting the fillet as you work.

Poached Cod with Dill Scallion Sauce

two ¾-inch-thick cod or scrod steaks
   (about 1 pound total)
¼ cup minced fresh dill
¼ cup minced scallion
1 tablespoon distilled white vinegar
1½ tablespoons drained bottled horseradish,
   or to taste
¼ cup olive oil

In a deep heavy skillet large enough to hold the cod steaks in one layer combine the steaks with enough salted cold water to cover them by 1 inch, bring the water to a simmer, and poach the steaks, covered, at a bare simmer for 5 to 6 minutes, or until they just flake. While the steaks are poaching, in a blender purée the dill and the scallion with the vinegar, the horseradish, the oil, and salt and pepper to taste. Transfer the steaks with a slotted spatula, draining them well, to plates and spoon the sauce over them. Serves 2.

Halibut Steaks with Oil and Lemon Dressing

2 tablespoons fresh lemon juice
¼ teaspoon dried orégano, crumbled
¼ teaspoon salt
2 tablespoons olive oil plus additional oil for
   brushing the fish
two 6-ounce halibut or cod steaks,
   each cut 1¼ inches thick
minced fresh parsley leaves for garnish

In a small bowl combine the lemon juice, the orégano, and the salt, add the 2 tablespoons oil in a stream, whisking, and whisk the dressing until it is emulsified. Brush both sides of the halibut with the additional oil and broil the halibut under a preheated broiler

about 2 to 3 inches from the heat for 3 to 4 minutes on each side, or until it just flakes. Transfer the halibut to a heated platter, spoon the dressing over it, and garnish the halibut with the fresh parsley. Serves 2.

Red Snapper with Tomato and Tarragon

2 tablespoons finely chopped shallot
1 tablespoon white-wine vinegar
1 tablespoon fresh lemon juice
2 tablespoons water
1 hard-boiled large egg yolk
3 tablespoons unsalted butter, melted
1 plum tomato, seeded and chopped
1½ teaspoons minced fresh tarragon
   or ½ teaspoon dried, crumbled
two 6- to 7-ounce red snapper fillets with
   the skin
2 lemon slices

In a small saucepan combine the shallot, the vinegar, the lemon juice, the water, and salt and pepper to taste, bring the mixture to a simmer, and simmer it, stirring occasionally, until the liquid is reduced to about 2 tablespoons. Transfer the mixture to a blender, add the egg yolk, and blend the mixture for 3 seconds. With the motor running add the butter, heated, in a stream, blend the sauce until it is combined well, and season it with salt and pepper. Pour the sauce into a small bowl, stir in the tomato and the tarragon, and keep it warm.

Sprinkle the fillets lightly with salt, arrange them skin sides down in a non-stick skillet, and put a lemon slice on each fillet. Cook the fillets, covered tightly, over moderately low heat for 8 to 10 minutes, or until they just flake, transfer them to heated plates, and spoon the sauce over them. Serves 2.

Grilled Salmon Steaks with Soy and Lime

2 teaspoons fresh lime juice
2 tablespoons soy sauce
¾ teaspoon sugar
⅛ teaspoon salt
1 tablespoon vegetable oil
2 salmon steaks (1 pound), each about
   1 inch thick
lime wedges for garnish

In a bowl stir together the lime juice, the soy sauce, the sugar, the salt, and the oil and rub the mixture onto both sides of each salmon steak. Let the salmon stand for 15 minutes. Heat an oiled ridged grill pan over moderately high heat until it is smoking and in it sauté the salmon for 3 to 4 minutes on each side, or until it just flakes and is cooked through. Transfer the salmon to heated plates and serve it with the lime wedges. Serves 2.

Marinated Salmon Seared in a Pepper Crust

2 tablespoons soy sauce
1 garlic clove, pressed in a garlic press or
   minced and mashed to a paste
2 teaspoons fresh lemon juice
1 teaspoon sugar
¾ pound center-cut salmon fillet, skinned
   and halved
4 teaspoons coarsely ground black pepper
2 tablespoons olive oil

In a sealable plastic bag combine well the soy sauce, the garlic, the lemon juice, and the sugar, add the salmon, coating it well, and let it marinate, sealed and chilled, for 30 minutes. Remove the salmon from the bag, discarding the marinade, pat it dry, and press 2 teaspoons of the black pepper onto each piece of salmon, coating it thoroughly. In a heavy skillet heat the olive oil over moderately high heat until it is hot but not smoking and in it sauté the salmon for 2 minutes on each side, or until it just flakes.

Transfer the salmon with a slotted spatula to paper towels and let it drain for 30 seconds. Serves 2.

Photo on page 68

Poached Scrod with Herbs and Warm Vinaigrette

1 tablespoon white-wine vinegar
2 tablespoons extra-virgin olive oil
1 shallot, chopped fine
¼ cup finely chopped fresh mint leaves
¼ cup finely chopped fresh basil leaves
¼ cup finely chopped fresh parsley leaves
two ½-pound pieces scrod fillet

In a small saucepan combine the vinegar, the oil, the shallot, and salt and pepper to taste. In a small bowl combine well the mint, the basil, and the parsley and on each of 2 plates mound one fourth of the herb mixture. In a deep skillet bring 1 inch of salted water to a boil, add the scrod, skinned sides down, and poach it, covered, at a bare simmer for 8 minutes, or until it just flakes. Transfer each fillet with a slotted spatula, blotting it with paper towels and reserving the cooking liquid, to a bed of herbs and top the scrod with the remaining herb mixture. Add 1 tablespoon of the reserved cooking liquid to the vinegar mixture, bring the mixture to a boil, and spoon it over the scrod. Serves 2.

Photo on page 32

Sole with Cabbage and Mustard Butter Sauce

4 cups thinly sliced cabbage
1½ tablespoons Dijon-style mustard
1 tablespoon white-wine vinegar
1 tablespoon medium-dry Sherry
½ pound sole or flounder fillets
½ cup milk
seasoned flour for dredging the sole
¼ cup vegetable oil
3 tablespoons unsalted butter
2 scallions, sliced thin and separated into rings, for garnish

In a kettle of boiling salted water blanch the cabbage for 1 minute, drain it, and transfer it to a platter. Keep the cabbage warm in a pre-heated 200° F. oven, covered loosely. In a bowl whisk together the mustard, the vinegar, and the Sherry. In another bowl dip the sole in the milk and dredge it in the seasoned flour, shaking off the excess. In a large heavy skillet heat the oil over moderately high heat until it is hot and in it sauté the sole in batches, turning it once, for 2 to 3 minutes, or until it just flakes. Transfer the sole with a slotted spatula to paper towels, let it drain briefly, and arrange it on the cabbage. Pour off the oil from the skillet and wipe the skillet clean with paper towels.

In the skillet cook the butter over moderately high heat, swirling the skillet occasionally, until the foam subsides and the butter is nut-brown and whisk in the mustard mixture. Pour the sauce over the sole and garnish the sole with the scallion rings. Serves 2.

Sole with Snow Peas and Red Onion in Lemon Vinaigrette

For the vinaigrette
2 tablespoons fresh lemon juice
1 teaspoon freshly grated lemon zest
1 teaspoon Dijon-style mustard
¼ cup olive oil

two 6-ounce sole fillets
white pepper to taste
¼ pound snow peas, trimmed, strings discarded, and cut diagonally into ½-inch pieces, plus 6 small whole snow peas for garnish
½ small red onion, sliced thin lengthwise
a 3-inch-long strip of lemon zest removed with a vegetable peeler and cut lengthwise into fine julienne strips
thin strips of lemon zest, tied decoratively, for garnish

Sole with Snow Peas and Red Onion in Lemon Vinaigrette

Make the vinaigrette: In a small bowl whisk together well the lemon juice, the zest, the mustard, and salt to taste, add the oil in a stream, whisking, and whisk the vinaigrette until it is emulsified.

Season the fillets with salt and the white pepper, arrange them in a buttered jelly-roll pan, and bake them, their surface covered with a buttered piece of foil, in a preheated 400° F. oven for 7 minutes, or until they barely flake. While the fillets are baking, in a saucepan of boiling salted water blanch the cut and whole snow peas for 5 seconds, drain them in a colander, and refresh them under cold water. Transfer the sole fillets carefully with a slotted spatula to 2 plates, sprinkle them with the cut snow peas, drained and patted dry, the onion, and the julienne zest, and spoon the vinaigrette over them. Let the fillets stand for 5 minutes, or until they are room temperature, and garnish the plates with the whole snow peas, patted dry, and the tied lemon strips. Serves 2.

Photo on this page

Sole Cakes

¾ pound sole fillets
¼ cup minced onion
3 tablespoons minced celery
2 tablespoons minced green bell pepper
1 tablespoon minced fresh parsley leaves
1 tablespoon minced scallion
1 large egg
1 tablespoon milk
1½ cups fine fresh bread crumbs
1 teaspoon salt
¼ teaspoon cayenne
fine dry bread crumbs for coating the cakes
3 tablespoons vegetable oil
drained bottled horseradish as an
  accompaniment

In a food processor chop the sole fillets coarse. In a bowl combine the sole with the onion, the celery, the bell pepper, the parsley, the scallion, the egg, the milk, the fresh bread crumbs, the salt, and the cayenne, form the mixture into four 3¼-inch cakes, and coat the cakes with the dry bread crumbs.

In a large skillet heat the oil over moderately high heat until it is hot, in it sauté the cakes for 2 minutes on each side, or until they are golden brown, and transfer them with a slotted spatula to paper towels to drain. Arrange the sole cakes on a heated platter and serve them with the horseradish. Serves 2.

Sole Paupiettes with Orange Rosemary Butter Sauce

two 6- to 8-ounce sole fillets, the thicker
  end of each fillet flattened slightly between
  dampened sheets of plastic wrap
freshly ground white pepper to taste
½ cup dry white wine or dry vermouth
2 cups water
1 tablespoon minced shallot
¼ teaspoon salt

For the sauce
2 tablespoons minced shallot
¼ cup white-wine vinegar
¼ cup dry white wine or dry vermouth
1 teaspoon freshly grated orange zest
¼ cup fresh orange juice
1 tablespoon minced fresh rosemary leaves
1 tablespoon cold water
½ stick (¼ cup) cold unsalted butter,
  cut into bits

For the garnish
peeled halved orange slices
blanched julienne strips of orange zest
rosemary sprigs

Arrange the fillets, skinned sides up, on a work surface and season them with salt and the white pepper. Cut each fillet lengthwise into thirds. Beginning with the narrow (tail) end of each piece, roll up the pieces jelly-roll fashion and secure them with wooden picks. In a buttered skillet just large enough to hold the *paupiettes* in one layer combine the wine, the water, the shallot, the salt, and white pepper to taste and bring the liquid to a simmer. Arrange the *paupiettes*, cut sides up, in the skillet and poach them, covered with a buttered round of wax paper, at a bare simmer for 4 to 6 minutes, or until they flake when tested with a fork and are no longer translucent in the center. Transfer the *paupiettes* with a slotted spatula to paper towels to drain and keep them warm, covered, on 2 dinner plates.

Sole Paupiettes with Orange Rosemary Butter Sauce

Make the sauce: In a small heavy saucepan combine the shallot, the vinegar, the wine, the zest, the orange juice, and the rosemary and cook the mixture over moderately high heat until the liquid is reduced to about 2½ tablespoons. Strain the mixture through a fine sieve into the pan, pressing hard on the solids, and add the water. Whisk in the butter, 1 piece at a time, over low heat, lifting the pan from the heat occasionally to cool the mixture and adding each new piece of butter before the previous one has melted completely. (The sauce must not get hot enough to liquefy.) Season the sauce with salt and white pepper.

Spoon a pool of sauce around the *paupiettes* and garnish the plates with the orange slices, the zest, and the rosemary sprigs. Serves 2.

Photo on this page

Steamed Sole with Ginger Sauce

two 6-ounce sole fillets
1 ounce boiled ham, cut into julienne strips

For the sauce
a piece of gingerroot, 2½ by 1 by ¼ inch,
  peeled and cut into julienne strips
1 small garlic clove, minced
1½ teaspoons olive oil
1½ teaspoons cider vinegar
1 teaspoon soy sauce
¼ teaspoon sugar
¼ teaspoon cornstarch

Arrange the sole on a heatproof serving dish and sprinkle it with the ham. Put the dish in a steamer set over boiling water, steam the sole and the ham, covered, for 3 minutes, and reserve the liquid that accumulates in the dish.

Make the sauce: In a small skillet cook the gingerroot and the garlic in the oil over moderately low heat, stirring occasionally, until they are softened, add the reserved liquid, and boil it over moderately high heat until it is reduced to about ¼ cup. In a small bowl combine the vinegar and the soy sauce and stir in the sugar and the cornstarch, stirring until they are dissolved. Whisk the vinegar mixture into the ginger mixture, cook the mixture over moderately high heat, stirring, for 2 to 3 minutes, or until it is thickened, and spoon it over the sole. Serves 2.

Foil-Baked Swordfish with Fennel, Olives, and Orange

1 fennel bulb* (about ¼ lb), trimmed and cut
  into julienne strips, reserving 2 tablespoons
  of the fennel sprigs, chopped, if desired
1 tablespoon unsalted butter
4 oil-cured Kalamata olives, pitted and
  sliced thin

1 teaspoon freshly grated orange zest
2 tablespoons dry white wine or
  dry vermouth
1½ teaspoons fresh lemon juice
two 6-ounce swordfish steaks
  (about ¾ inch thick)

*sometimes called anise, available in most
  supermarkets

In a heavy skillet cook the fennel strips in the butter over moderate heat, stirring occasionally, for 5 to 6 minutes, or until they are crisp-tender, add the olives, the zest, the wine, the lemon juice, and salt and pepper to taste and cook the mixture, stirring, for 1 to 2 minutes, or until the liquid is reduced slightly. Fold 2 pieces of 20- by 12-inch foil in half by bringing the short ends together, unfold each piece, and arrange a swordfish steak, seasoned with salt and pepper, just to one side of each fold line. Top the swordfish with the fennel mixture and sprinkle the fennel mixture with the reserved fennel sprigs if desired. Fold the foil over the swordfish to enclose them, fold the edges together to form tightly sealed packets, and bake the packets on a baking sheet in a preheated 450° F. oven for 10 minutes. Transfer the packets to plates and slit them open at the table or alternatively open the packets carefully, transfer the swordfish and fennel mixtures to plates, and pour the juices over the swordfish and fennel mixture, discarding the foil. Serves 2.

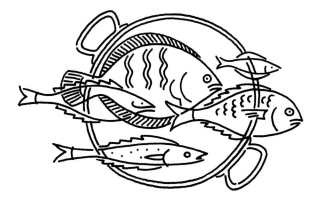

Sautéed Swordfish with Green Olives and Capers Vinaigrette

3½ tablespoons olive oil
two 1-inch-thick swordfish steaks
¼ cup finely chopped Spanish olives
　　with pimiento
1 tablespoon finely chopped fresh parsley
　　leaves, preferably flat-leafed
1 tablespoon drained bottled capers,
　　chopped fine
1 small garlic clove, minced and mashed
　　to a paste with ¼ teaspoon salt
2 tablespoons minced scallion
½ tablespoon balsamic or red-wine vinegar
lemon wedges as an accompaniment

In a skillet, preferably non-stick, heat 1½ table-spoons of the oil over moderately high heat until it is hot but not smoking and in it sauté the swordfish steaks, patted dry, for 4 to 5 minutes on each side, or until they are just cooked through. While the fish is cooking, in a bowl stir together the olives, the parsley, the capers, the garlic paste, the scallion, the vinegar, the remaining 2 tablespoons oil, and salt and pepper to taste. Transfer the swordfish to plates, spoon the sauce over it, and serve it with the lemon wedges. Serves 2.

Steamed Fish Fillets with Shiitake Mushrooms and Ginger

6 ounces fresh shiitake mushrooms, stems
　　discarded, cut into ¼-inch julienne strips
2 tablespoons vegetable oil
a 1½-inch-long piece of fresh gingerroot,
　　peeled and cut into fine julienne strips
2 large scallions, cut into julienne strips
¾-pound white fish fillets
1 teaspoon Oriental sesame oil
soy sauce to taste as an accompaniment
white-wine vinegar to taste as an
　　accompaniment

In a skillet cook the mushrooms with salt and pepper to taste in the oil over moderate heat, stirring, until the liquid they give off is evaporated. Stir in the gingerroot and the scallions and stir-fry the mixture for 2 minutes. Let the mixture cool.

　Sprinkle the fish fillets on both sides with salt and pepper. Sprinkle the fillets on the skinned side with half the mushroom mixture, and fold each fillet in half to enclose the mixture. Arrange the fillets in a steamer set over boiling water and steam them, covered, for 3 minutes, or until they are opaque and just flake. Transfer the fillets to a platter and keep them warm, covered. Reheat the remaining mushroom mixture over moderate heat, stir in the sesame oil, and spoon the mixture over the fillets. Serve the fish sprinkled with the soy sauce and the vinegar. Serves 2.

Spicy Steamed Clams with Fennel

SHELLFISH

Shellfish, as distinguished from finfish, carry their skeletons on the outside of their bodies. Our recipes include a mix of crustaceans (crabs, lobsters, and shrimp) and mollusks (clams, mussels, oysters, and scallops) in a variety of quick preparations.

All shellfish are extremely perishable (even more so than finfish), so always make sure that they are fresh when purchased and buy them the same day you plan to serve them. Here are some guidelines:

Crabs and lobsters, ideally, should be purchased live straight from your fishmonger's marine tanks. Make sure that these crustaceans are lively when purchased and still lively at cooking time.

Shrimp, peeled or not, should be firm and completely intact (not broken into pieces). They should always look bright, shiny, moist, and translucent.

Clams, mussels, and oysters should have tightly closed and unbroken shells to indicate that they are alive. If, however, the shells are slightly open but close after a hard knock, this means the mollusks are still alive. A heavy shell probably indicates that it is filled with sand or mud, and it should be discarded.

Scallops are usually shucked at sea, which means that they are no longer alive by the time we buy them. They should, however, be shiny and firm and should smell sweet.

Steamers in Beer with Dill Dipping Sauce

12 ounces beer (not dark)
½ cup water
3½ tablespoons cold unsalted butter
5½ teaspoons minced fresh dill
2½ pounds steamers (soft-shelled clams), scrubbed
2 teaspoons fresh lemon juice

In a large saucepan combine the beer, the water, ½ tablespoon of the butter, 4 teaspoons of the dill, and the steamers, bring the liquid to a boil, and steam the steamers, covered, over moderately high heat, shaking the pan occasionally, for 5 to 10 minutes, or until they are opened. Divide the steamers with a slotted spoon between 2 bowls, reserving the cooking liquid, and keep them warm, covered.

In a small saucepan heat 2 tablespoons of the reserved cooking liquid and the lemon juice over low heat and whisk in the remaining 3 tablespoons butter, 1 tablespoon at a time, adding each new piece before the previous one has melted completely. Season the dipping sauce with the remaining 1½ teaspoons dill and salt and pepper to taste, divide it between 2 small bowls, and divide some of the remaining cooking liquid between 2 other bowls. Serve the steamers with the bowls of cooking liquid and dipping sauce. Serves 2 as a light luncheon.

Spicy Clams Casino

3 slices of lean bacon, each cut crosswise into fourths
3 tablespoons unsalted butter, softened
2 tablespoons minced scallion
1 *jalapeño* chili, seeded and minced (wear rubber gloves)
12 medium hard-shelled clams, shucked (procedure follows), reserving the bottom shells
lemon juice to taste

In a skillet cook the bacon over moderate heat, turning it once, until it is golden but still soft, transfer it to paper towels to drain, and reserve it. In a small bowl stir together the butter, the scallion, the *jalapeño*, and salt and pepper to taste. Arrange the reserved clam shells in a baking pan just large enough to hold them in one layer and divide the butter mixture among them. Top the butter mixture with the clams, sprinkle the clams with the lemon juice, and top each clam with a piece of the reserved bacon. Bake the clams in the middle of a preheated 450° F. oven for 10 minutes. Serves 2.

To Shuck Hard-Shelled Clams

Scrub the clams thoroughly with a stiff brush under cold water, discarding any that have cracked shells or that are not shut tightly.

Wearing an oven mitt and working over a bowl to reserve the liquor, hold each clam in

the palm of the hand with the hinge against the heel of the palm. Force a clam knife between the shells, cut around the inside edges to sever the connecting muscles, and twist the knife slightly to open the shells.

Spicy Steamed Clams with Fennel

1 large garlic clove, minced
¼ teaspoon dried hot red pepper flakes,
**   or to taste**
¾ teaspoon dried orégano, crumbled
2 tablespoons olive oil
½ cup finely chopped onion
1¼ cups thinly sliced fennel bulb (sometimes
**   called anise, available in most supermar-**
**   kets), or celery combined with ½ teaspoon**
**   fennel seeds**
a 14-ounce can plum tomatoes, drained,
**   reserving the juice, and chopped**
½ cup dry white wine or dry vermouth
24 small hard-shelled clams, scrubbed well
2 tablespoons minced fresh parsley leaves
**   plus parsley sprigs for garnish**
crusty bread as an accompaniment

In a heavy saucepan cook the garlic, the pepper flakes, and the orégano in the oil over moderately low heat, stirring, for 1 minute, add the onion and the fennel, and cook the mixture over moderate heat, stirring, until the fennel is softened. Add the tomatoes with the reserved juice, the wine, and salt and pepper to taste and simmer the mixture, uncovered, stirring occasionally, for 5 minutes. Add the clams, steam them, covered, for 5 to 7 minutes, or until they have opened, and discard any unopened clams. Transfer the clams to a serving dish, stir the minced parsley into the fennel mixture, and spoon the mixture over the clams. Garnish the clams with the parsley sprigs and serve them with the bread. Serves 2.

Photo on page 78

Red and Green Bell Pepper Crab Cakes

1 small garlic clove, minced
¼ cup finely chopped green bell pepper
¼ cup finely chopped red bell pepper
3 tablespoons unsalted butter
¼ cup plus 2 tablespoons crushed
**   saltine crackers**
1 large egg, beaten lightly
2 tablespoons minced scallion
2 teaspoons fresh lemon juice
1 teaspoon Worcestershire sauce
a pinch of cayenne
1 tablespoon mayonnaise
½ pound lump crab meat, picked over
all-purpose flour for coating the crab cakes
1 tablespoon vegetable oil
tartar sauce as an accompaniment
lemon wedges as an accompaniment

In a small skillet cook the garlic and the bell peppers in 2 tablespoons of the butter over moderately low heat, stirring, for 2 minutes, or until they are softened. Transfer the mixture to a bowl, add the cracker crumbs, the egg, the scallion, the lemon juice, the Worcestershire sauce, the cayenne, and the mayonnaise, and combine the mixture well. Add the crab meat, stirring lightly until the mixture is just combined, and let the mixture stand, covered, for 10 minutes. Form the crab mixture into four ½-inch-thick cakes and coat the cakes with the flour. In a large heavy skillet heat the oil and the remaining 1 tablespoon butter over moderately high heat until the foam subsides. Add the crab cakes to the skillet and cook them, turning them carefully, for 3 to 4 minutes on each side, or until they are golden brown. Serve the crab cakes with the tartar sauce and the lemon wedges. Makes 4 crab cakes, serving 2 as a main course.

Steamed Mussels in Mustard and Parsley Sauce

1½ pounds mussels
1 onion, chopped
2 tablespoons vegetable oil
2 garlic cloves, minced
2 tablespoons dry white wine or
  dry vermouth
¼ cup sour cream
2 tablespoons fresh bread crumbs
1 to 2 tablespoons Dijon-style mustard, or
  to taste
2 tablespoons minced fresh parsley leaves

Scrub the mussels well in several changes of water, scrape off the beards, and rinse the mussels. In a kettle cook the onion in the oil over moderately low heat, stirring, until it is softened. Add the garlic, the mussels, and the wine and steam the mussels, covered, for 3 to 5 minutes, or until they are opened. Transfer the mussels as they open with a slotted spoon to a heated dish and cover them with a hot dampened kitchen towel to keep them from drying out. Discard any unopened mussels. Add the sour cream and the bread crumbs to the kettle, bring the liquid to a boil, and boil the mixture over high heat for 3 to 5 minutes, or until the sauce is thickened. Stir the mustard and the parsley into the sauce, add the mussels, stirring to coat them with the sauce, and divide the mixture between 2 heated bowls. Serves 2.

Lobster in Spicy Tomato Sauce with Coriander

½ cup thinly sliced shallot
1 tablespoon unsalted butter
1 tablespoon olive oil
a 2- to 2½-pound live lobster
1½ pounds tomatoes, peeled, seeded, and
  chopped coarse
¼ cup dry white wine or dry vermouth
1 teaspoon dried hot red pepper flakes
2 tablespoons tequila
2 tablespoons minced fresh coriander

In a large deep skillet cook the shallot in the butter and the oil over moderately low heat, stirring occasionally, until it is softened. While the shallot is cooking, cook the lobster: Into a kettle of boiling salted water plunge the lobster and boil it, covered, for 8 minutes. Transfer the lobster to a work surface and let it cool until it can be handled. To the skillet add the tomatoes, the wine, the red pepper flakes, and salt and black pepper to taste, bring the mixture to a boil, stirring, and boil it for 5 minutes, or until it is thickened. While the sauce is cooking, pull the lobster tail apart from the body and stir 2 tablespoons of the tomalley and any roe from the tail and body sections into the sauce. With a cleaver, cut the tail section crosswise through the shell into medallions, separate the claws and joints, and crack the shells of the claws and joints with the back of the cleaver. Add the lobster (discarding the body section) and the tequila to the skillet, simmer the lobster mixture, stirring, for 1 minute, and sprinkle the coriander over it. Serves 2.

Oysters and Eggplant Louisiana

7 tablespoons olive oil
1 small eggplant (about 8 ounces), peeled
  and sliced crosswise into ½-inch-thick slices
1 tablespoon unsalted butter
½ cup minced onion
¼ cup minced green bell pepper
½ teaspoon minced garlic
12 oysters, shucked (procedure follows),
  reserving the liquor
¾ cup fine fresh bread crumbs
1 tablespoon thinly sliced scallion
cayenne to taste
⅔ cup freshly grated Parmesan

In a large heavy skillet heat 4 tablespoons of the oil over moderately high heat until it is hot but not smoking, in it sauté the eggplant in batches, turning it once, for 2 to 3 minutes, or until it is browned well, and drain it on paper towels. To the skillet add 1 tablespoon of the remaining oil and the butter and sauté the onion and the bell pepper over moderately high heat until they are browned. Stir in the garlic and sauté the mixture for 1 minute. Add the reserved oyster liquor, reduce the liquid to about ½ cup, and stir in the bread crumbs, the scallion, the cayenne, and salt to taste.

In a buttered gratin dish arrange the eggplant in one layer, spoon the oysters over it, and cover the mixture with the bread crumb mixture. Sprinkle the mixture with the Parmesan and drizzle it with the remaining 2 tablespoons oil. Bake the dish in a preheated 375° F. oven for 7 minutes and broil it under the broiler about 3 to 4 inches from the heat for 3 to 4 minutes, or until it is browned. Serves 2.

To Shuck Oysters

Scrub the oysters thoroughly with a stiff brush under cold water and break off the thin end of the shells. Hold each oyster in the palm of the hand with the hinged end facing you, force an oyster knife between the shells at the broken end, and twist it to force the shells apart, cutting the large muscle close to the flat upper shell. Break off and discard the flat shell and slide the knife under the oyster to release it.

Oyster Po' Boys with Guacamole and Shredded Lettuce

1 California avocado
2 scallions, chopped fine
1 plum tomato, seeded and chopped fine
2 teaspoons fresh lemon juice
1 large egg
2 tablespoons milk
vegetable oil for deep-frying the oysters
12 shucked oysters (procedure on this page), drained
flour for dredging the oysters
two 6-inch pieces of French or Italian bread
1 cup shredded iceberg lettuce

Peel and pit the avocado and, using a fork, mash it coarsely in a bowl. Stir in the scallions, the tomato, the lemon juice, and salt and pepper to taste. In another bowl whisk together the egg and the milk. In a large deep skillet heat 1 inch of the oil to 375° F. Dip the oysters in the egg mixture, dredge them in the flour, shaking off the excess, and fry them in the oil for 1 to 2 minutes, or until they are golden and crisp. Transfer the oysters with a slotted spoon to paper towels to drain. Cut each piece of bread horizontally with a serrated knife, not cutting all the way through. Divide the guacamole between the sandwiches, top it with the lettuce, and top the lettuce with the oysters. Serves 2.

Grilled Sea Scallops with Broccoli Rabe and Sun-Dried Tomatoes

½ pound pencil-thin broccoli rabe, washed,
    any yellow leaves and coarse stem ends
    discarded, and cut into 1-inch pieces
1 tablespoon olive oil
1 tablespoon unsalted butter
1 small garlic clove, minced
2 tablespoons minced drained sun-dried
    tomatoes
2 teaspoons fresh lemon juice
¾ pound sea scallops
vegetable oil for brushing the scallops

In a large heavy skillet cook the broccoli rabe in the olive oil and the butter, covered, over moderate heat, stirring occasionally, for 5 minutes, or until it is crisp-tender. Stir in the garlic, the sun-dried tomatoes, the lemon juice, and salt and pepper to taste and cook the mixture, stirring, for 1 minute. Transfer the broccoli rabe mixture to a platter and keep it warm, covered. Heat a well-seasoned ridged grill pan over moderately high heat until it begins to smoke, in it grill the scallops, brushed lightly with the vegetable oil, for 1½ to 2 minutes on each side, or until they are just cooked through, and arrange them on the broccoli rabe. (Alternatively, the scallops can be sautéed in the heavy skillet.) Serves 2.

Scallops with Tarragon and Chives

3 tablespoons unsalted butter
¾ pound sea scallops, rinsed, patted dry, and
    quartered
1 garlic clove, minced
3 tablespoons minced shallot
2 tablespoons minced fresh chives
2 teaspoons minced fresh tarragon or
    ¾ teaspoon dried, crumbled
1 teaspoon fresh lemon juice

In a heavy skillet heat 1½ tablespoons of the butter over moderately high heat until the foam subsides, in it sauté the sea scallops in batches for 1 minute, and transfer them to a plate. To the skillet add the remaining 1½ tablespoons butter and in it cook the garlic and the shallot over moderately low heat, stirring, until the shallot is softened. Stir in the chives, the tarragon, the lemon juice, the scallops, and salt and pepper to taste and heat the mixture, stirring, until the scallops are just heated through. Serves 2.

Bay Scallops with Tomato Garlic Sauce

1 garlic clove, minced
2 tablespoons unsalted butter
¾ pound bay scallops
¼ cup dry white wine or dry vermouth
2 plum tomatoes, seeded and chopped
1½ teaspoons fresh minced tarragon or
    ½ teaspoon dried, crumbled
2 tablespoons minced fresh parsley leaves
⅛ teaspoon freshly grated lemon zest,
    or to taste
Italian bread as an accompaniment

In a heavy skillet cook the garlic in the butter over moderately low heat, stirring occasionally, for 1 minute, increase the heat to high, and cook the garlic, stirring, until it is pale golden. Add the scallops, patted dry, cook them, stirring occasionally for 1½ to 2 minutes, or until they are just firm, and transfer them with a slotted spoon to a platter. Add the wine, the tomatoes, and the tarragon to the pan juices, boil the mixture, stirring, until it is reduced to about ¼ cup, and season the sauce with salt and pepper to taste. Remove the pan from the heat, stir in the parsley, the scallops, and the lemon zest, and serve the scallops with the bread. Serves 2.

Fried Shrimp with Crab Meat

6 large shrimp
3 tablespoons minced green bell pepper
3 tablespoons minced onion
1 tablespoon unsalted butter
¼ pound lump crab meat, picked over and
   flaked
1 large egg, beaten lightly
2 tablespoons milk
3 tablespoons thinly sliced scallion greens
½ cup fine fresh bread crumbs
⅛ teaspoon cayenne, or to taste
fine dry bread crumbs for dredging the shrimp
vegetable oil or shortening for deep-frying
   the shrimp
1 lemon, cut crosswise into 6 slices
   for garnish
tartar sauce as an accompaniment if desired

Shell the shrimp, leaving the tails and the last joint of the shells intact. Cut down the back of each shrimp with a sharp knife to butterfly it, devein the shrimp, and press each shrimp gently, cut side up, to flatten it.

In a small heavy skillet cook the bell pepper and the onion in the butter over moderately low heat until the vegetables are softened. In a bowl combine well the vegetable mixture, the crab meat, the egg, the milk, the scallion greens, the fresh bread crumbs, the cayenne, and salt to taste. Pat the shrimp dry, mold 2 rounded tablespoons of the crab meat mixture around each shrimp, and dredge the shrimp in the dry bread crumbs. In a deep skillet or deep fryer fry the shrimp in 2 inches of 360° F. oil for 2 to 3 minutes, or until they are golden brown, transfer them to paper towels to drain, and arrange them on the lemon slices on a platter. Serve the shrimp with the tartar sauce if desired. Serves 2.

Open-Faced Fried Shrimp Sandwiches with Ginger Mayonnaise

¾ pound small shrimp (about 36), shelled
all-purpose flour seasoned with salt
   and cayenne
vegetable oil for deep-frying the shrimp
2 tablespoons minced peeled fresh gingerroot
⅔ cup mayonnaise
3 tablespoons Dijon-style mustard
4 slices of rye bread, toasted lightly
10 radishes, trimmed and sliced thin
1 cup lightly packed alfalfa sprouts
4 watercress sprigs for garnish
2 teaspoons fresh lemon juice, or to taste

In a plastic bag, toss the shrimp with the seasoned flour to coat them, transfer the shrimp to a large sieve, and shake off the excess flour. In a kettle heat 1 inch of the oil over moderately high heat until it registers 375° F. on a deep-fat thermometer and in it fry the shrimp in batches, stirring occasionally, for 1 minute, or until they are just cooked through, transferring them as they are fried to paper towels to drain.

In a bowl stir together the gingerroot, the mayonnaise, and the mustard until the mixture is combined well and spread 1 tablespoon of the ginger mayonnaise on each piece of toast. Arrange the radishes, the alfalfa sprouts, and the shrimp decoratively on the toast and tuck a watercress sprig into each sandwich. Stir the lemon juice into the remaining mayonnaise and serve the sandwiches with the mayonnaise drizzled over them. Serves 2.

Photo on page 24

Shrimp with Garlic Sauce

6 tablespoons olive oil
1 garlic clove, minced
4 teaspoons minced fresh parsley leaves
3 tablespoons fresh lemon juice
⅓ cup medium-dry Sherry
¾ pound large shrimp, shelled with the tails left intact and deveined

In a skillet heat the oil until it is hot but not smoking, add the garlic and 2 teaspoons of the parsley, and cook the mixture over moderately high heat until the garlic is browned lightly. Stir in the lemon juice, the Sherry, and salt and freshly ground pepper to taste, add the shrimp, and cook them, stirring, for 4 to 6 minutes, or until they are just firm. Transfer the shrimp to a heated platter, spoon the sauce over them, and sprinkle the dish with the remaining 2 teaspoons parsley. Serves 2.

Bell Pepper Filled with Shrimp, Feta, and Pasta Salad

4 whole scallions plus 2 tablespoons thinly sliced scallion greens
2 teaspoons white-wine vinegar
4 teaspoons olive oil
¼ pound small shrimp (about 12), shelled and deveined
3 tablespoons orzo (rice-shaped pasta)
3 tablespoons crumbled Feta
1 large green bell pepper, quartered and the stem, seeds, and ribs discarded

Trim the root ends and the loose green parts of the whole scallions, leaving about 4 inches of firm scallion. Fringe the green ends with a sharp knife by cutting two 3-inch slits and rolling the scallion 90° for the second slit. Drop the scallion brushes as they are cut into a bowl of ice and cold water and chill them to curl the ends while making the salad.

In a small bowl whisk together the vinegar and salt and pepper to taste, add the oil, whisking, and whisk the dressing until it is emulsified. In a saucepan of boiling salted water boil the shrimp for 20 to 30 seconds, or until they are just firm to the touch, and drain them. Reserve 2 of the shrimp, halved lengthwise, for the garnish and chop the remaining shrimp. In a large saucepan of boiling salted water boil the *orzo* for 10 to 12 minutes, or until it is *al dente*. Drain the *orzo* in a sieve, refresh it under cold water, and drain it well. In a bowl combine the chopped shrimp, the *orzo*, the Feta, the sliced scallion greens, and salt and pepper to taste. Whisk the dressing, add it to the shrimp mixture, and toss the salad well.

Divide the salad among the pepper quarters, top each quarter with 1 of the reserved shrimp halves, and arrange the filled bell pepper quarters on a platter. Garnish the platter with the scallion brushes, drained well and patted dry carefully. Serves 2 as a light luncheon entrée.

Photo on page 87

Shrimp Timbales with Red Pepper Sauce

For the timbales
¼ cup chopped red bell pepper
¼ cup chopped green bell pepper
¾ pound shrimp, shelled and deveined
1 large egg
¾ cup well-chilled heavy cream
1 teaspoon salt, or to taste

For the sauce
1 cup finely chopped red bell pepper
1 tablespoon minced shallot
2 tablespoons unsalted butter
½ cup heavy cream

parsley sprigs for garnish

Bell Pepper Filled with Shrimp, Feta, and Pasta Salad

Make the timbales: In a large saucepan of boiling salted water blanch the red and green bell peppers for 3 minutes, drain them, and refresh them under cold water. Drain the peppers on paper towels and squeeze them gently to remove any excess water. In a food processor purée the shrimp with the egg, the cream, the salt, and pepper to taste until the mixture is a coarse purée and fold in the bell peppers.

Divide the mixture among 4 well-buttered ½-cup timbale molds or custard cups, cover the timbales with buttered foil, and put them in a baking pan. Pour enough hot water into the pan to reach halfway up the sides of the timbales and bake the timbales in a preheated 350° F. oven for 15 minutes, or until a metal skewer comes out clean.

Make the sauce: In a saucepan cook the bell pepper and the shallot in the butter, covered, over moderately high heat, stirring occasionally, until the pepper is softened. Add the cream, bring the mixture to a gentle boil, stirring, and boil it until it thickens slightly. Season the sauce with salt and pepper and purée it in a blender.

Remove the foil and invert the shrimp timbales onto a heated platter. Blot up any excess liquid, garnish the tops with the parsley sprigs, and spoon the sauce around the timbales. Serves 2.

Filets Mignons with Pearl Onions and Artichokes

MEAT

Here you will find smaller cuts of meat that can be quickly sautéed, grilled, or broiled. In order to prepare meat dishes, you should have a few basic pieces of equipment:

A heavy wooden board that will not slide as you prepare and slice meat. This meat board should have a ridge or a well to collect juices, but don't be tempted to buy a board with prongs that hold the meat in place. The prongs drain the meat of its juices and make it difficult to position the meat for slicing.

Top quality knives for carving, boning, and slicing. High carbon no-stain steel knives are an excellent choice because they keep a sharp edge and do not rust. A good knife is well-balanced with a comfortable handle. The blade should be riveted to the handle, not bonded with glue.

A heavy skillet that will cook the meat evenly. You should invest in a pan that is well-balanced with a sturdy and secure handle. Cast-iron skillets are excellent, as are aluminum pans lined with stainless steel.

And, there are a few other pans that you might consider. A cast-iron ridged grill pan is a great piece of equipment if you do not have access to an outdoor grill, or in cases of inclement weather. The pan's lengthwise ridges create the same attractive grill marks, and you can cook without added fat. This pan works well with fish and poultry too. And, you may want a wok if you do a lot of stir-fry cooking. With just a tablespoon or two of oil this large, bowl-shaped pan allows you to fry your meats and accompanying vegetables in minutes.

Beef and Veal
🍎 🍎 🍎

Grilled Flank Steak

2 tablespoons vegetable oil
1½ tablespoons fresh lime juice
1 tablespoon soy sauce
a 1-inch piece of peeled fresh gingerroot,
    chopped fine
1 garlic clove, minced
a ¾-pound flank steak, scored lightly on
    both sides
lime wedges for garnish

In a shallow dish just large enough to hold the
steak whisk together the oil, the lime juice, the
soy sauce, the gingerroot, and the garlic, add
the steak, coating both sides well with the
marinade, and let it marinate, turning it once,
for 20 minutes.

Remove the steak from the marinade and
grill it on an oiled rack over glowing coals,
brushing it occasionally with some of the
marinade, for 4 to 5 minutes on each side for
medium-rare meat. Alternatively, broil the
steak on the rack of a broiler pan under a preheated broiler about 4 inches from the heat,
for 5 to 7 minutes on each side for medium-
rare meat. Transfer the steak to a platter and
let it stand for 10 minutes. Holding a sharp
knife at a 45° angle slice the steak thin across
the grain. Garnish the steak with the lime
wedges. Serves 2.

Filets Mignons with Pearl Onions and Artichokes

3 tablespoons unsalted butter, softened
1 tablespoon minced red bell pepper
a pinch of dried thyme, crumbled
2 teaspoons minced watercress leaves plus
    watercress sprigs for garnish
1 cup pearl onions, blanched in boiling water
    for 5 minutes and peeled
3 canned artichoke bottoms, drained and cut
    crosswise into ¼-inch slices
1 tablespoon vegetable oil
2 filets mignons, each 1½ inches thick

In a small bowl stir together 2 tablespoons of the
butter, the bell pepper, the thyme, and 1 teaspoon of the watercress and chill the mixture. In
a small skillet cook the pearl onions, the artichokes, and the remaining 1 teaspoon watercress
in the remaining 1 tablespoon butter with salt
and pepper to taste over moderate heat, stirring,
until the mixture is heated through, transfer the
mixture to a bowl, and keep it warm. In the skillet heat the oil over moderately high heat until it
is hot but not smoking, add the filets, patted dry
and seasoned with salt and pepper, and sauté
them for 6 to 7 minutes on each side for rare
meat. Transfer the filets to heated plates and top
each filet with half the butter mixture. Spoon half
the onion mixture onto each plate and garnish
the plates with the watercress sprigs. Serves 2.

Photo on page 88

Chicken-Fried Steak Strips with Milk Gravy

1 large egg
½ cup milk
3 tablespoons chopped onion, pressed
    through a garlic press, reserving the pulp
    and the juice
1 garlic clove, pressed through a garlic press
½ pound round steak, cut into strips, 4 by
    ½ by ½ inch
seasoned flour for dredging the steak strips
vegetable oil for frying the steak strips

For the gravy
1½ teaspoons flour
1 cup milk at room temperature

In a bowl whisk together the egg, the milk, the onion pulp and juice, and the garlic, dip the steak strips into the mixture, and dredge them in the seasoned flour, shaking off the excess. In a large heavy skillet heat ½ inch of the oil over moderately high heat until it is hot, in it fry the steak strips in batches, turning them once, for 3 minutes, and transfer them to paper towels to drain. Keep the strips warm on an ovenproof platter in a preheated 200° F. oven.

Make the gravy: Pour off the oil from the skillet, reserving 2 tablespoons of it, and wipe the skillet clean. In the skillet cook the flour in the reserved oil over moderate heat, stirring, for 5 minutes, add the milk in a stream, whisking, and simmer the gravy, whisking, for 5 minutes. Transfer the gravy to a sauceboat.

Divide the steak strips between 2 heated serving plates and nap them with the gravy. Serves 2.

Stir-Fried Beef with Red Bell Peppers and Snow Peas

For the beef
2 teaspoons soy sauce
¼ teaspoon sugar
1 teaspoon Oriental sesame oil
¼ teaspoon salt
¾ pound boneless sirloin, cut across the grain into ¼-inch-thick slices

For the sauce
1 tablespoon cornstarch
1 tablespoon soy sauce
1 tablespoon medium-dry Sherry or Scotch
⅓ cup chicken or beef broth or water
2 teaspoons Oriental sesame oil
1½ teaspoons rice vinegar or white-wine vinegar
¾ teaspoon sugar

3 tablespoons vegetable oil
1 tablespoon minced peeled fresh gingerroot
1 tablespoon minced garlic
a 4-inch fresh red chili, seeded and minced (wear rubber gloves) or ½ teaspoon dried hot red pepper flakes
¼ pound snow peas, trimmed, strings discarded
1 red bell pepper, cut into ¼-inch strips
cooked rice as an accompaniment

Prepare the beef: In a small bowl stir together the soy sauce, the sugar, the sesame oil, and the salt, add the beef, and let it marinate for 20 minutes.

Make the sauce while the beef is marinating: In a small bowl dissolve the cornstarch in the soy sauce and stir in the Sherry, the broth, the sesame oil, the vinegar, and the sugar.

Heat a wok or large heavy skillet over high heat until it is hot, add 2 tablespoons of the vegetable oil, and heat it until it just begins to smoke. Stir-fry the beef, patted dry, in the oil in batches for 1 minute, or until it is no longer pink, and transfer it as it is cooked with a slotted spoon to a plate. Add the remaining 1 tablespoon vegetable oil to the wok, heat it until it is hot but not smoking, and in the oil stir-fry the gingerroot, the garlic, and the chili for 30 seconds, or until the mixture is fragrant. Add the snow peas and the bell pepper and stir-fry the mixture for 1 minute. Stir the sauce, add it to the wok with the beef and any juices that have accumulated on the plate, and cook the mixture, stirring, for 2 minutes, or until the sauce is thickened and the beef is heated through. Transfer the mixture to a heated platter and serve it with the rice. Serves 2.

Steak Diane

two ½-inch-thick (about 6 ounces each) sirloin
     steaks, trimmed and flattened ¼ inch thick
1 tablespoon olive oil
2 tablespoons unsalted butter
2½ tablespoons minced shallot
2 teaspoons fresh lemon juice, or to taste
1 teaspoon Worcestershire sauce
1 teaspoon cornstarch
½ cup beef broth
2 tablespoons minced fresh parsley leaves
1 teaspoon Cognac

In a large heavy skillet sauté the steaks, patted dry, in the oil and 1 tablespoon of the butter over moderately high heat, turning them once, for 1½ minutes and transfer them to heated plates. Add the remaining 1 tablespoon butter to the skillet, sauté the shallot in it over moderately high heat, stirring, until the shallot is browned, and stir in the lemon juice and the Worcestershire sauce. In a bowl dissolve the cornstarch in the broth, stir the mixture and the parsley into the skillet, and cook the mixture over moderately high heat until it is thickened. Whisk in the Cognac and salt and pepper to taste and spoon the sauce over the steaks. Serves 2.

Grilled Skirt Steak with Parsley Jalapeño Sauce

2 tablespoons minced fresh parsley leaves
1 small garlic clove, minced and mashed to a
     paste with ¼ teaspoon salt
2 small pickled *jalapeño* chilies, or to taste,
     seeded and minced to a paste (wear
     rubber gloves)
2 tablespoons olive oil
¾ to 1 pound skirt steak, halved crosswise

In a small bowl stir together the parsley, the garlic paste, the *jalapeños*, the oil, and salt and

pepper to taste until the mixture is combined well. Grill the steak, seasoned generously with salt and pepper, on an oiled rack set about 6 inches over glowing coals for 4 minutes on each side for medium-rare meat. Transfer the steak to a cutting board, let it stand for 5 minutes, and cut it across the grain into thin slices. Divide the steak between 2 plates, top it with some of the parsley jalapeño sauce, and serve the remaining sauce separately. Serves 2.

Photo on page 26

Tortillas with Steak and Tomato Salsa

4 flour tortillas

For the salsa
1 tomato, seeded and chopped
½ small red onion, chopped fine
two 2-inch pickled *jalapeño* chilies, seeded
     and chopped fine (wear rubber gloves)
¼ cup minced fresh coriander
1 tablespoon vegetable oil
¾ teaspoon Worcestershire sauce
¼ teaspoon salt, or to taste

1 tablespoon vegetable oil
½ pound boneless sirloin steak, cut across
     the grain into ¼-inch strips
¼ cup sour cream

Warm the tortillas, wrapped in foil, in a preheated 200° F. oven.

Make the salsa while the tortillas are warming: In a small bowl stir together the tomato, the onion, the *jalapeños*, the coriander, the vegetable oil, the Worcestershire sauce, and the salt.

In a large heavy skillet, heat the vegetable oil over moderately high heat until it is hot but not smoking, add the steak strips, patted dry, and cook them, stirring constantly, for 30 seconds to 1 minute, or until the strips are browned on the outside but still pink within for medium-rare meat. Divide the sour cream among the tortillas, spreading it evenly, add the steak and the salsa, and roll up each tortilla, enclosing the filling. Serves 2.

Open-Faced Burgers with Green Peppercorn and Tomato Relish

For the relish

1 onion, chopped fine

1 tablespoon vegetable oil

1 tomato, peeled, seeded, and chopped

½ teaspoon sugar

½ teaspoon salt

2 teaspoons drained green peppercorns in brine, chopped

¾ pound ground chuck

1 Kaiser or other hard roll, halved horizontally

Make the relish: In a small skillet cook the onion in the oil over moderate heat, stirring, until it is softened. Add the tomato, the sugar, and the salt and cook the mixture over moderately high heat, stirring, until it is thick. Remove the pan from the heat, stir in the green peppercorns, and let the relish cool.

Halve the chuck and shape each half into a ¾-inch-thick patty. Heat a well-seasoned cast-iron skillet over high heat until it begins to smoke, add the burgers, and reduce the heat to moderately high. Cook the burgers, covered, for 3 minutes on each side for medium-rare meat.

Arrange one half of the roll on each of 2 plates, set a burger on each half, and top it with some of the relish. Serve any remaining relish separately. Serves 2.

Calf's Liver with Mustard Sauce

2 slices of calf's liver, ¼ inch thick (about ½ pound)

seasoned flour for dredging the liver

¼ cup vegetable oil

½ small onion, minced

1 tablespoon unsalted butter

⅓ cup heavy cream

1 tablespoon Dijon-style mustard

3 tablespoons minced fresh parsley leaves

1 teaspoon fresh lemon juice

Dredge the liver in the seasoned flour, shaking off the excess. In a heavy skillet heat the oil over moderately high heat until it is hot but not smoking and in it sauté the liver, turning it once, for 2 minutes, or until it is browned on the outside but still pink within. Transfer the liver with tongs to a heat-proof platter and keep it warm in a preheated 200° F. oven. Discard the oil and wipe out the skillet. In the skillet cook the onion in the butter over moderately low heat, stirring, until it is softened, add the cream, and boil it until it is just thickened. Remove the skillet from the heat, stir in the mustard, the parsley, the lemon juice, and salt and pepper to taste, and spoon the sauce over the liver. Serves 2.

93

Veal Chop "Schnitzel" with Arugula Salad

Veal Chop "Schnitzel" with Arugula Salad

two 1-inch-thick veal rib chops, frenched
flour seasoned with salt and pepper for
 dredging the chops
1 large egg, beaten lightly
¾ cup fine fresh bread crumbs
1 large garlic clove, quartered
¼ cup vegetable oil
1 tablespoon unsalted butter

For the salad
1 tablespoon white-wine vinegar
1 teaspoon Dijon-style mustard
⅛ teaspoon dried thyme, crumbled

2 tablespoons olive oil
2 cups loosely packed *arugula* or watercress
 sprigs, washed well and spun dry
4 cherry tomatoes, quartered
1 tablespoon grated carrot

2 lemon wedges for garnish

Pound the meat of the chops ½ inch thick
between sheets of plastic wrap, being careful
not to separate the meat from the bone, pat it
dry, and season it with salt and pepper. Dredge
the chops in the seasoned flour, shaking off
the excess, dip them in the egg, letting the
excess drip off, and coat them with the bread
crumbs. In a large heavy skillet cook the garlic
in the oil and the butter over moderately high

heat, stirring, until it is golden and discard it. Sauté the chops in the fat, turning them once, for 4 minutes, or until they are golden brown, and transfer them to paper towels to drain.

Make the salad: In a small bowl whisk together the vinegar, the mustard, the thyme, and salt and pepper to taste, add the oil in a stream, whisking, and whisk the dressing until it is emulsified. In a bowl toss the *arugula*, the tomatoes, and the carrot with the dressing.

Arrange each veal chop on a plate, divide the salad between the plates, and garnish each serving with a lemon wedge. Serves 2.

Photo on page 94

Veal Paprika

8 teaspoons vegetable oil
½ pound veal cutlets, flattened ⅛ inch thick between sheets of plastic wrap
flour seasoned with salt and pepper for dredging the veal
1 onion, sliced thin
1 garlic clove, minced
2 teaspoons sweet paprika
½ cup plus 2 tablespoons sour cream
¾ cup water
1 teaspoon fresh lemon juice, or to taste
2 teaspoons minced fresh parsley leaves

In a heavy skillet heat 2 tablespoons of the oil over moderately high heat until it is hot but not smoking and in it brown the veal, patted dry and dredged in the seasoned flour, in batches, transferring it as it is browned to a plate. Discard any oil remaining in the skillet and wipe the skillet out carefully with paper towels. Add the remaining 2 teaspoons oil to the skillet and in it cook the onion over moderate heat, stirring, until it is golden. Stir in the garlic, the paprika, ½ cup of the sour cream, the veal and any juices that have accumulated on the platter, and the water, bring the liquid to a boil, stirring, and simmer the veal, covered, for 15 to 20 minutes, or until it is tender and the

sauce is thickened. Stir in the remaining 2 tablespoons sour cream, the lemon juice, and salt and pepper to taste and sprinkle the dish with the parsley. Serves 2.

Veal Scallops with Mushroom Herb Sauce

2 tablespoons olive oil
¾ pound veal scallops, pounded thin between sheets of plastic wrap
½ cup chicken broth
2 tablespoons minced shallot
3 mushrooms (about 2 ounces), minced
1 tablespoon snipped fresh chives
2 tablespoons minced fresh tarragon leaves or 2 teaspoons dried, crumbled
2 tablespoons minced fresh parsley leaves
2 teaspoons fresh lemon juice
2 tablespoons cold unsalted butter, cut into bits

In a large skillet heat the oil over moderately high heat until it is hot but not smoking, in it sauté the veal, patted dry and seasoned with salt and pepper, in batches, for 30 to 45 seconds on each side, or until it is browned lightly, and transfer it with tongs to a plate. Pour off the fat from the skillet, add the broth, and deglaze the skillet over high heat, scraping up the brown bits. Add the shallot, the mushrooms, the chives, the tarragon, and the parsley and boil the mixture until it is reduced by two thirds. Add the lemon juice, the butter, and salt and pepper to taste and simmer the mixture, swirling the skillet, until the butter is just melted. Return the veal to the skillet with any juices that have accumulated on the plate and turn the veal to coat it with the sauce. Divide the veal between 2 heated plates and nap it with the sauce. Serves 2.

Pork
ಟ ಟ ಟ

Pork Tenderloin with Pears and Rosemary Cream Sauce

a ¾-pound pork tenderloin, cut crosswise
    into 1-inch slices, reserving 3 inches of
    the narrow end for another use
2 tablespoons unsalted butter
2 small pears
2 shallots, minced
½ teaspoon dried rosemary, crumbled,
    or to taste
¼ cup apple cider or apple juice
2 tablespoons fresh lemon juice
½ cup chicken broth
¼ cup heavy cream

Flatten the pork slices, cut sides up, to about ¼-inch thickness between sheets of plastic wrap. In a large heavy skillet heat 1 tablespoon of the butter over moderately high heat until the foam begins to subside. In the butter sauté the pork, patted dry and seasoned with salt and pepper, in batches, turning it once, for 4 minutes. Transfer the pork with tongs to a platter and keep it warm, covered. Peel and core the pears and cut each one into 8 wedges. In the skillet cook the pear wedges in the remaining 1 tablespoon butter, covered, over moderately high heat, turning them once, for 2 minutes, or until they are golden and just tender. Transfer the pear wedges with tongs to the platter of pork and keep them warm, covered. Add the shallots to the skillet and cook them over moderate heat, stirring, for 2 minutes. Add the rosemary, the cider, and the lemon juice, deglaze the skillet, scraping up the brown bits, and boil the liquid, stirring occasionally, until it is reduced to about 2 tablespoons. Add the broth and boil the mixture, stirring, until the liquid is reduced by half. Add the cream and the pork with any juices that have accumulated on the platter, leaving the pears on the platter, and boil the mixture, stirring and turning the pork occasionally, for 1 minute, or until the sauce is thickened slightly. Transfer the pork with tongs to the platter and pour the sauce over it. Serves 2.

Pork Loin with Vegetable Mélange

1 small rib of celery with the leaves, chopped
1 garlic clove, halved
1 small onion, quartered
¼ cup chopped green bell pepper
⅛ teaspoon cayenne, or to taste
½ teaspoon salt
½ pound whole boneless pork loin, butterflied
    and halved crosswise
½ cup water

In a food processor or blender purée the celery, the garlic, the onion, and the bell pepper, transfer the purée to a small bowl, and stir in the cayenne and the salt.

Broil the pork halves in a flameproof pan under a preheated broiler about 5 to 6 inches from the heat for 10 minutes, turn them, and spread them with two thirds of the vegetable purée, spooning the remaining purée around them. Broil the pork for 8 to 10 minutes more, or until a meat thermometer registers 150° F., and transfer it to a heated serving dish. To the pan add the water, bring it to a boil, scraping up the brown bits, and reduce the liquid over high heat to about ⅓ cup. Strain the sauce into a small bowl, pressing hard on the solids, and spoon it around the pork. Serves 2.

Stir-Fried Pork with Romaine

2 teaspoons soy sauce
2 teaspoons medium-dry Sherry
2 teaspoons distilled white vinegar
1 tablespoon cornstarch
1¼ pounds loin pork chops, boned, cut into
  ¼-inch strips, and the fat removed
¼ cup slivered blanched almonds
1½ tablespoons vegetable oil
8 cups (about 1 head) loosely packed
  shredded romaine
½ cup water
fresh lemon juice to taste

Marinate the pork: In a bowl combine the soy sauce, the Sherry, and the vinegar and dissolve the cornstarch in the mixture. Add the pork to the bowl, tossing it to coat it with the marinade, and let it marinate for 5 minutes.

While the pork is marinating, in a wok or heavy skillet cook the almonds in 1½ teaspoons of the oil over moderate heat, stirring, for 2 to 3 minutes, or until they are golden, and transfer them to paper towels to drain. In the wok heat 1½ teaspoons of the remaining oil over moderately high heat until it is hot, in it stir-fry the romaine for 1 minute, or until it is just wilted but still crisp, and transfer the romaine to a heated platter.

Heat the remaining 1½ teaspoons oil in the wok over moderately high heat until it is hot, in it stir-fry the pork with the marinade until the pork is no longer pink, and transfer the mixture to the platter. Add the water to the wok and deglaze the wok over moderately high heat, scraping up the brown bits, until the mixture has thickened. Spoon the sauce over the pork and romaine, add salt to taste if desired, and toss the dish to combine it. Sprinkle the dish with the almonds and the lemon juice. Serves 2.

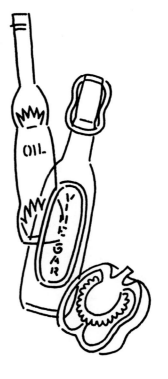

Pork Chops with Mustard

1½ teaspoons Dijon-style mustard
1 teaspoon fresh lemon juice
¼ teaspoon salt, or to taste
two ½-inch-thick center-cut pork chops
2 tablespoons seasoned fine fresh bread
  crumbs

In a small bowl whisk together the mustard, the lemon juice, the salt, and pepper to taste, arrange the pork chops on a broiler pan lightly brushed with oil, and brush the tops with half the mustard mixture. Broil the chops under a preheated broiler about 4 inches from the heat for 5 minutes, turn them, and brush the tops with the remaining mustard mixture. Broil the chops for 5 minutes, sprinkle the tops with the bread crumbs, and broil the chops for 1 minute, or until the tops are golden brown. Serves 2.

Barbecued Spareribs

2 pounds lean pork spareribs, cut into
  individual ribs
¼ cup ketchup
2 tablespoons firmly packed light brown sugar
2 tablespoons fresh lemon juice
1 tablespoon soy sauce
¾ teaspoon Worcestershire sauce, or to taste
⅛ teaspoon cayenne

In a kettle simmer the ribs in salted water for
30 minutes and drain them. While the ribs are
cooking, in a small saucepan combine the
ketchup, the brown sugar, the lemon juice, the
soy sauce, the Worcestershire sauce, the
cayenne, and freshly ground black pepper to
taste, bring the basting sauce to a boil, stirring,
and simmer it for 5 minutes. Arrange the ribs,
meaty side up, on the oiled rack of a broiler
pan, brush them with some of the basting
sauce, and broil them under a preheated broiler
about 4 inches from the heat for 5 to 7 minutes, or until they are browned. Brush the ribs
with the remaining basting sauce. Serves 2.

Kielbasa with Peppers, Onions, and Mashed Potatoes

1 tablespoon vegetable oil
¾ pound smoked *kielbasa* (Polish sausage),
  cut into 1-inch pieces
1 yellow bell pepper, cut into ¼-inch strips
1 red bell pepper, cut into ¼-inch strips
1 onion, sliced thin
½ cup water, plus 2 tablespoons hot water
¾ pound yellow-fleshed or russet (baking)
  potatoes
¼ cup milk, scalded
1 scallion, minced
1 tablespoon unsalted butter, cut into bits

In a large heavy skillet heat the oil over moderate heat until it is hot but not smoking and in
it brown the *kielbasa*. Add the bell peppers and
the onion and cook the mixture, stirring, for
1 minute. Add the ½ cup water and simmer
the mixture, covered partially, for 10 minutes,
or until the vegetables are tender.

While the *kielbasa* mixture is simmering,
in a steamer set over boiling water steam the
potatoes, peeled and cut into ¾-inch pieces,
covered, for 12 minutes, or until they are very
tender, transfer them to a bowl, and mash
them with a potato masher. Beat in the milk,
the 2 tablespoons hot water, the scallion, the
butter, and salt and pepper to taste and stir the
potato mixture until the butter is melted.
Serve the *kielbasa* mixture on the mashed
potatoes. Serves 2.

Broiled Ham Steak with Sweet and Spicy Mustard Sauce

a 1-pound ham steak (about ¹/₂ inch
  thick), the edge scored at 1-inch intervals
2 tablespoons currant jelly
2 tablespoons Dijon-style mustard
⅛ teaspoon cayenne

Rinse the ham, pat it dry, and set it on the
rack of a broiler pan. In a small saucepan heat
the currant jelly over moderate heat, stirring
occasionally, until it is melted and whisk in the
mustard and the cayenne. Brush the ham
lightly with half of the sauce and broil it under
a preheated broiler about 4 inches from the
heat for 4 minutes. Turn the ham steak, brush
it with the remaining sauce, and broil it for
4 minutes, or until the meat is heated through
and the top is lightly browned. Serves 2.

Lamb
❧ ❧ ❧

Lamb Medallions with Red and Green Bell Peppers

four ¾-inch-thick loin lamb chops, boned and tied into medallions
seasoned flour for dredging the lamb
1 tablespoon olive oil
1 red bell pepper, cut into julienne strips
1 green bell pepper, cut into julienne strips
¼ cup dry white wine or dry vermouth, or to taste

In a dish dredge the lamb in the seasoned flour, shaking off the excess. In a heavy skillet heat the oil over moderately high heat until it is hot but not smoking and in it sauté the lamb for 3 minutes on each side for medium-rare meat. Transfer the lamb to a heated platter and discard the string. In the skillet sauté the bell peppers with salt and pepper to taste over moderately high heat for 2 to 3 minutes, or until they are crisp-tender, and arrange them around the lamb. Deglaze the skillet with the wine over high heat, scraping up the brown bits, and spoon the sauce over the lamb medallions and the peppers. Serves 2.

Rack of Lamb with Tarragon Lemon Sauce

a 1¼-pound trimmed and frenched single rack of lamb (7 or 8 ribs)
1 tablespoon unsalted butter
1 teaspoon freshly grated lemon zest
2 teaspoons minced fresh tarragon or ¾ teaspoon dried, crumbled, plus tarragon sprigs for garnish
1 tablespoon fresh lemon juice

Heat an ovenproof skillet over moderately high heat until it is hot and in it brown the lamb, seasoned with salt and pepper, turning it, for 4 minutes, or until the sides and the ends are browned evenly. Pour off any fat from the skillet, arrange the lamb, fat and meat side up, and bake it in the middle of a preheated 475° F. oven for 15 minutes, or until a meat thermometer registers 130° F. for medium-rare meat. Transfer the lamb carefully to a cutting board, and let it stand, uncovered, for 10 minutes. While the lamb is standing, in a small saucepan melt the butter and stir in the zest, the minced tarragon, the lemon juice, and salt and pepper to taste.

Cut the lamb between the ribs and divide it between 2 plates. Garnish the lamb with the tarragon sprigs and serve it with the sauce. Serves 2.

Photo on front jacket

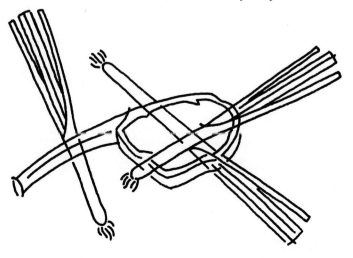

Rack of Lamb with Rosemary Scallion Crust; Curried Couscous and Bell Pepper Timbales

Rack of Lamb with Rosemary Scallion Crust

1½ tablespoons olive oil
¼ teaspoon dried hot red pepper flakes
1 garlic clove, minced
3 tablespoons thinly sliced scallion including the green part
1 teaspoon dried rosemary, crumbled
½ cup fresh bread crumbs
a 1¼-pound trimmed and frenched single rack of lamb (7 or 8 ribs)
watercress sprigs for garnish if desired

In a small skillet heat the oil over moderate heat until it is hot but not smoking, add the red pepper flakes, and cook them, stirring, for 10 seconds. Add the garlic and cook it, stirring, for 30 seconds. Add the scallion and the rosemary and cook the mixture, stirring, for 10 seconds. Stir in the bread crumbs and salt and pepper to taste and remove the skillet from the heat.

Heat an ovenproof skillet over moderately high heat until it is hot and in it brown the lamb, seasoned with salt and pepper, turning it, for 5 minutes, or until the sides and the ends are browned evenly. Pour off any fat from the skillet, arrange the lamb, fat and meat side up, and pat the crumb mixture evenly on the fat and meat side of the lamb. Bake the lamb in the middle of a preheated 475° F. oven for 15 minutes, or until a meat thermometer registers 130° F. for medium-rare meat. Transfer the lamb to a platter, let it stand, uncovered, for 10 minutes, and garnish it with the watercress. Serves 2.

Photo on page 100

Moroccan-Style Lamb Sauté with Tomato and Prune Sauce

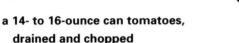

a 14- to 16-ounce can tomatoes,
   drained and chopped
½ teaspoon cinnamon
⅛ teaspoon ground cloves
¼ teaspoon crumbled saffron threads
   if desired
2 ounces pitted prunes (⅓ cup packed)
¼ cup water
1 tablespoon olive oil
4 small 1-inch-thick rib lamb chops

In a saucepan combine the tomatoes, the cinnamon, the cloves, the saffron, half the prunes, quartered, and the water, simmer the mixture, stirring occasionally, for 20 minutes, and season the sauce with salt and pepper.

In a heavy skillet heat the oil over moderately high heat until it is hot but not smoking, add the chops, patted dry and seasoned with salt and pepper, and sauté them for 3 to 4 minutes on each side for medium-rare meat. Divide the lamb chops between 2 heated plates, spoon the sauce over them, and garnish the dish with the remaining prunes, cut into ¼-inch pieces. Serves 2.

Lamb Patties with Coriander Mint Sauce

¾ pound ground lamb (not too lean)
3 tablespoons minced scallion
a pinch of cinnamon
⅛ teaspoon ground cumin

For the sauce
½ cup plain yogurt
1 tablespoon minced fresh coriander
1 tablespoon minced fresh mint leaves or
   1 teaspoon dried, crumbled, or to taste
½ teaspoon minced garlic

romaine, rinsed and spun dry, for lining
   the plates
pita loaves, halved, as an accompaniment
   if desired

In a bowl combine the lamb, the scallion, the cinnamon, the cumin, and salt and pepper to taste, knead the mixture with your hands until it is combined well, and chill it, covered, for 15 minutes. Form the lamb mixture into four 1-inch-thick patties. On the lightly oiled rack of a broiler pan broil the patties under a preheated broiler about 4 inches from the heat for 4 to 5 minutes on each side for medium-rare meat.

Make the sauce while the lamb is broiling: In a bowl whisk together the yogurt, the coriander, the mint, the garlic, and salt and pepper to taste.

Divide the patties between 2 plates lined with the romaine and serve them with the yogurt sauce and the *pita* loaves. Serves 2.

Chicken Roasted with Potatoes, Peppers, and Shallots

POULTRY

Poultry is inexpensive, nutritious, and delicious. Most of our recipes call for chicken breasts because they offer ready-made individual portions that can be cooked quickly in various ways. We have also included a few easy recipes for chicken legs and thighs, Cornish game hens, and turkey cutlets.

When shopping for chicken and turkey pieces, look for plump meat and be sure to check the package for the freshness date. Gently squeeze the package to see if the meat is properly chilled but free of ice.

You may want to try free-range poultry. A good breeder gives these birds plenty of space to roam and a vegetarian diet free of hormones and growth-enhancers. The result, while more expensive, is a fuller-tasting bird. Try Bell and Evans, available in many butcher shops, or call D'Artagnan, at 800-327-8246 for overnight delivery.

No doubt you have heard about the dangers of salmonella in poultry, but if you take the following precautions there is no need to worry. Proper storage, handling, and cooking are imperative. Keep poultry chilled to 40° F. or below until you are ready to cook it. Hands, utensils, boards—*everything* that comes in contact with poultry preparation—should be washed in warm soapy water before it comes in contact with other foods. Cook your poultry thoroughly and check for doneness by piercing a small piece in its thickest part with a skewer; the juices should run clear. Cooked poultry should never sit at room temperature for longer than two hours.

Chicken
❦ ❦ ❦

Almond-Crusted Chicken Breast with Pears and Roquefort

1 whole skinless boneless chicken breast
  (about ½ pound), halved lengthwise and
  flattened slightly between sheets
  of plastic wrap
flour seasoned with salt and pepper for
  dredging the chicken
1 large egg, beaten lightly
¾ cup sliced natural almonds
2 tablespoons vegetable oil
2 tablespoons minced shallot
1 small pear
¼ cup dry white wine or dry vermouth
¼ cup heavy cream
2 tablespoons crumbled Roquefort

Dredge the chicken in the seasoned flour, shaking off any excess, dip it in the egg, and coat it with the almonds. In a large heavy skillet heat the oil over moderate heat until it is hot but not smoking, in it cook the chicken, turning it once, for 4 to 6 minutes on each side, or until it is golden and just cooked through, and transfer it with tongs to an oven-proof platter, letting the excess oil drip off. Keep the chicken warm in a preheated 200° F. oven. Pour off the oil in the skillet, add the shallot, and the pear, peeled, cored, and cut into ¼-inch slices, and cook them over moderate heat, stirring, for 1 minute. Add the wine and boil it until it is reduced by half. Stir in the cream, the Roquefort, and salt and pepper to taste, cook the sauce, stirring, until it is thickened, and ladle it around the chicken. Serves 2.

Braised Chicken with Artichoke Hearts and Sun-Dried Tomatoes

1 tablespoon olive oil
1 whole chicken breast with the skin
  (about 1½ pounds), halved
½ cup finely chopped onion
1 tablespoon minced garlic
¼ cup dry white wine or dry vermouth
½ cup chicken broth
a 14-ounce can artichoke hearts, rinsed,
  drained, and quartered
¼ cup drained sun-dried tomatoes
  (packed in oil), sliced thin
a *beurre manié* made by kneading together
  1 tablespoon softened unsalted butter and
  1 tablespoon all-purpose flour
2 tablespoons minced fresh basil leaves

In a heavy skillet heat the oil over moderately high heat until it is hot but not smoking, in it brown the chicken, patted dry and seasoned with salt and pepper, and transfer the chicken to a plate. In the fat remaining in the skillet cook the onion and the garlic over moderately low heat, stirring, until the onion is softened. Add the wine, the broth, the artichoke hearts, the sun-dried tomatoes, and the chicken and simmer the mixture, covered, for 15 to 20 minutes, or until the chicken is springy to the touch and just cooked through. Transfer the chicken to a platter and keep it warm. Whisk the *beurre manié* into the artichoke mixture and simmer the sauce, whisking, for 2 to 3 minutes, or until it is thickened. Stir in the basil and pour the sauce over the chicken. Serves 2.

Grilled Chicken with Spicy Corn and Sun-Dried Tomato Salsa ◇4◇

For the salsa
½ cup cooked corn kernels (from about 1 ear)
2 tablespoons minced drained sun-dried
    tomatoes (packed in oil)
3 tablespoons thinly sliced scallion
1 garlic clove, minced and mashed to a paste
    with ¼ teaspoon salt
1 teaspoon minced seeded fresh *jalapeño*
    chili, or to taste (wear rubber gloves)
1½ tablespoons fresh lime juice
1 tablespoon olive oil
2 to 3 tablespoons finely chopped fresh
    coriander, or to taste
½ teaspoon ground cumin

1 whole boneless chicken breast with the
    skin (about 1 pound), halved and flattened
    slightly between sheets of plastic wrap
olive oil for brushing the chicken

Make the salsa: In a bowl stir together the corn, the sun-dried tomatoes, the scallion, the garlic paste, the *jalapeño*, the lime juice, the oil, the coriander, the cumin, and salt and pepper to taste.

Brush the chicken with the oil, season it with salt and pepper, and grill it on a rack set 5 to 6 inches over glowing coals or in a hot well-seasoned ridged grill pan, covered, over moderately high heat, for 4 to 6 minutes on each side, or until it is springy to the touch and just cooked through. Divide the chicken and the salsa between 2 plates. Serves 2.

Chicken Paillards with Herbs ◇4◇

1 whole skinless boneless chicken breast
    (about 10 ounces), halved and flattened
    ¼ inch thick between sheets of plastic wrap
2 garlic cloves
¼ cup chicken broth
1 tablespoon chopped fresh parsley leaves
1 tablespoon chopped fresh chives
1 tablespoon chopped fresh basil leaves
fresh lemon juice to taste
1 tablespoon olive oil

In a dish chill the chicken for 25 minutes. In a small saucepan combine the garlic and the broth, bring the broth to a boil, and boil the garlic for 3 minutes. In a blender purée the garlic and the broth with the herbs, the lemon juice, and salt and pepper to taste. Transfer the sauce to the pan and keep it warm. In a large heavy skillet heat the oil over moderately high heat until it is hot but not smoking and in it sauté the chicken, seasoned with salt and pepper, for 2 minutes on each side, or until it is springy to the touch and just cooked through. Serve the *paillards* with the sauce. Serves 2.

Fried Chicken Breast with Mustard Mayonnaise

◆4◆

**1 whole skinless boneless chicken breast
(about ¾ pound), halved and flattened ⅓ inch
thick between sheets of plastic wrap**
½ cup buttermilk
¼ cup mayonnaise
1 teaspoon fresh lemon juice
1½ teaspoons whole-grain mustard
1 cup all-purpose flour
2 teaspoons salt
1½ teaspoons freshly ground black pepper
1 teaspoon paprika (preferably Hungarian)
3 tablespoons vegetable oil

In a bowl let the chicken stand in the buttermilk, turning it occasionally, for 30 minutes. In another bowl stir together the mayonnaise, the juice, and the mustard. In a shallow dish stir together the flour, the salt, the black pepper, and the paprika and dredge the chicken in the flour mixture. Dip the chicken back into the buttermilk and dredge it again in the flour mixture, making sure that it is coated well. In a skillet heat the oil over moderately high heat until it is hot but not smoking and in it pan-fry the chicken, for 3 to 4 minutes on each side, or until it is springy to the touch and just cooked through. Serve the chicken with the mustard mayonnaise. Serves 2.

Pan-Grilled Chicken with Spicy Black Olives and Red Onion

◆4◆

¾ teaspoon minced and mashed garlic
3 tablespoons fresh lemon juice
3 tablespoons olive oil
**1 whole boneless chicken breast with the skin
(about 1 pound)**
¼ cup Kalamata olives, pitted and sliced
¼ cup finely chopped red onion
2 tablespoons minced fresh parsley leaves
¼ teaspoon dried hot red pepper flakes
2 lemon wedges for garnish

In a shallow dish whisk together ½ teaspoon of the garlic, 2 tablespoons of the lemon juice, 2 tablespoons of the oil, and salt to taste. Add the chicken, turning it to coat it with the marinade, and let it marinate, turning it once, for 20 minutes.

In a small bowl combine the olives, the remaining 1 tablespoon lemon juice, the remaining 1 tablespoon oil, the onion, the parsley, the red pepper flakes, the remaining ¼ teaspoon garlic, and salt to taste and toss the mixture until it is combined.

Heat a ridged grill pan or well-seasoned cast-iron skillet over moderate heat until it is hot and in it cook the chicken, skin side down, covered, for 4 minutes on each side, or until it is springy to the touch and just cooked through. Transfer the chicken to a cutting board and let it stand for 5 minutes. Halve the chicken lengthwise and holding the knife at a 45° angle cut each half crosswise into 1-inch slices. Transfer the chicken to heated plates, garnish each plate with the lemon wedges, and top the chicken with the olive mixture. Serves 2.

Braised Chicken with Onions, Bacon, and White Wine

◆4◆

2 slices of lean bacon
10 pearl onions
1 onion, chopped
1 garlic clove, minced
2 tablespoons unsalted butter
½ cup chicken broth
¼ cup dry white wine or dry vermouth
1½ teaspoons Worcestershire sauce
⅛ teaspoon dried thyme, crumbled
**1 whole skinless boneless chicken breast
(about ¾ pound), halved and flattened
slightly between sheets of plastic wrap**
mashed potatoes as an accompaniment

In a skillet cook the bacon over moderate heat until it is crisp and transfer it to paper towels to drain. Let the bacon cool and crumble it coarse. In a saucepan of boiling salted water cook the pearl onions for 5 minutes. Transfer the pearl onions to a bowl, let them cool, and peel them. Pour off the fat remaining in the skillet, and in it cook the chopped onion and the garlic in the butter, stirring, until they are softened. Add the chicken broth, the wine, the Worcestershire sauce, the thyme, and salt and pepper to taste and simmer the mixture for 3 minutes. Add the chicken, the bacon, and the pearl onions, baste them with the cooking liquid, and simmer the mixture, covered, for 10 minutes, or until the chicken is springy to the touch and just cooked through. Skim the fat from the sauce. Serve the chicken mixture with the mashed potatoes. Serves 2.

vegetable mixture. Roast the chicken and the vegetables in the upper third of a preheated 450° F. oven for 20 minutes, reduce the temperature to 375° F., and roast the chicken and vegetables for 15 minutes more, or until the chicken is springy to the touch and just cooked through and the potatoes are tender. Transfer the chicken and the vegetables with a slotted spoon to a heated platter, stir the broth into the skillet, scraping up the brown bits, and boil the mixture for 1 minute. Strain the liquid through a sieve over the chicken and garnish the chicken with the rosemary sprigs. Serves 2.

Photo on page 102

107

Chicken Roasted with Potatoes, Peppers, and Shallots

3 large shallots, peeled, blanched in boiling water for 2 minutes, and halved lengthwise
2 garlic cloves, minced
2 tablespoons plus 1 teaspoon olive oil
½ red bell pepper, cut into 1-inch pieces
½ yellow bell pepper, cut into 1-inch pieces
1 tablespoon finely chopped fresh rosemary leaves or 1 teaspoon dried, crumbled, plus, if desired, rosemary sprigs for garnish
¾ pound small red potatoes, scrubbed and halved or, if large, quartered
1 whole chicken breast with the skin (about 1½ pounds), halved
1 tablespoon fresh lemon juice
½ cup chicken broth

In a large ovenproof skillet toss together the shallots, the garlic, 2 tablespoons of the oil, the bell peppers, the chopped rosemary, the red potatoes, and salt and pepper to taste. Rub the chicken with the remaining 1 teaspoon oil, the lemon juice, and salt and pepper to taste and arrange it, skin sides up, on top of the

Chicken Breast with Prosciutto and Sage

**1 whole skinless boneless chicken breast
(about 10 ounces), halved lengthwise
and flattened slightly between sheets of
plastic wrap
flour seasoned with salt and pepper for
dredging the chicken
2 tablespoons unsalted butter
½ cup dry white wine or dry vermouth
¾ teaspoon dried sage, crumbled
2 ounces prosciutto or smoked ham
(about 2 slices), cut into julienne strips**

Dredge the chicken lightly in the seasoned flour. In a large skillet heat the butter over moderately high heat until the foam subsides and in it sauté the chicken, patted dry and seasoned with salt and pepper to taste, for 2 minutes on each side, or until it is browned lightly. Transfer the chicken with tongs to a heated plate and keep it warm, covered, in a preheated 250° F. oven.

To the skillet add the white wine and the sage, bring the liquid to a boil, stirring, and boil the mixture, scraping up the brown bits, for 1 minute. Add the chicken with any juices that have accumulated on the plate and the prosciutto, simmer the mixture, covered, for 4 to 5 minutes, or until the chicken is springy to the touch and just cooked through, and season it with salt and pepper. Transfer the chicken to 2 plates and spoon the prosciutto sauce over it. Serves 2.

Sesame Chicken with Stir-Fried Cabbage and Snow Peas

**1 whole boneless chicken breast with the
skin (1 pound), halved and flattened slightly
between sheets of plastic wrap
2 teaspoons sesame seeds
1 tablespoon vegetable oil**

**½ pound Napa cabbage, sliced thin (about
4 cups)
¼ pound snow peas, trimmed and strings
discarded
1 tablespoon white-wine vinegar
1 tablespoon soy sauce
1½ teaspoons Oriental sesame oil
1½ teaspoons minced peeled fresh gingerroot
¼ teaspoon sugar**

Season the chicken with salt and pepper and coat it with the sesame seeds. Heat a ridged grill pan or heavy skillet over moderately high heat until it is hot, brush it with oil, and in it sauté the chicken for 4 to 6 minutes on each side, or until it is springy to the touch and just cooked through.

While the chicken is cooking, in a large skillet heat the oil over moderately high heat until it is hot but not smoking and in it stir-fry the cabbage and the snow peas for 3 minutes, or until they are crisp-tender. In a small bowl combine well the vinegar, the soy sauce, the sesame oil, the gingerroot, and the sugar, add the mixture to the vegetables with salt and pepper to taste, and stir-fry the mixture over moderately high heat for 1 minute. Divide the vegetable mixture between 2 heated plates, cut the chicken against the grain into ¼-inch-thick slices, and arrange it on top of the vegetables. Serves 2.

Grilled Swiss Cheese and Chicken Sandwiches

**1½ tablespoons unsalted butter
1 whole skinless boneless small chicken
breast (about ¾ pound)
3 tablespoons mayonnaise
1 tablespoon ketchup
4 thick slices of rye bread
4 slices of Swiss cheese, cut to fit the bread
2 whole small sweet pickles, sliced thin,
plus 2 whole pickles for garnish
2 slices of red onion**

Grilled Swiss Cheese and Chicken Sandwiches

1 large egg
2 tablespoons milk

In a small heavy skillet heat ½ tablespoon of the butter over moderately high heat until the foam subsides, in it sauté the chicken, turning it once, for 12 to 15 minutes, or until it is springy to the touch and just cooked through, and on a work surface shred the chicken. In a small bowl combine well the mayonnaise, the ketchup, and salt and pepper to taste, divide the mixture among the bread slices, spreading it, and top it with the Swiss cheese. Divide the pickle and onion slices between 2 of the half-sandwiches, top them with the chicken, and cover the chicken with the remaining half-sandwiches.

In a small shallow dish whisk together the egg, the milk, and salt and pepper to taste, press each sandwich together firmly, and dip the sandwiches, 1 at a time, in the egg mixture, turning them to coat them thoroughly. In a heavy skillet heat ½ tablespoon of the remaining butter over moderate heat until the foam subsides and in it cook the sandwiches, covered, for 4 minutes, or until the undersides are golden brown. Turn the sandwiches carefully, add the remaining ½ tablespoon butter, and cook the sandwiches, covered, for 4 minutes more, or until the undersides are golden brown. Transfer the sandwiches to plates, halve them with a serrated knife, and garnish them with the whole pickles, cut lengthwise into fan shapes. Serves 2.

Photo on this page

Teriyaki-Style Chicken

2½ tablespoons soy sauce
½ teaspoon minced peeled fresh gingerroot
5 teaspoons honey
1 tablespoon medium-dry Sherry
1 tablespoon white-wine vinegar
1 garlic clove, minced and mashed to a paste
   with ½ teaspoon salt
1 whole boneless chicken breast with the skin
   (about 1 pound), halved and flattened ½ inch
   thick between sheets of plastic wrap

In a bowl whisk together the soy sauce, the gingerroot, the honey, the Sherry, the vinegar, and the garlic paste. Add the chicken and let it marinate in the soy mixture, turning it once, for 20 minutes.

Transfer the chicken, reserving the marinade in a small saucepan, skin sides down, to the oiled rack of a broiler pan and broil it under a preheated broiler about 6 inches from the heat for 5 minutes. While the chicken is cooking, boil the reserved marinade until it is reduced by half. Brush the chicken with some of the marinade, turn it, and brush it with the remaining marinade. Broil the chicken for 4 to 6 minutes more, or until it is springy to the touch and just cooked through, transfer it to a cutting board, and cut it on the diagonal into ½-inch-thick slices. Serves 2.

Photo on page 30

Spiced Walnut Chicken

½ cup walnuts, toasted lightly
2 whole chicken legs, cut into drumsticks
   and thighs (about 1 pound)
2 tablespoons olive oil
⅓ cup minced onion
¼ teaspoon turmeric
¼ cup chicken broth
1 teaspoon fresh lemon juice

1 tablespoon tomato paste
1½ tablespoons prepared jellied cranberry
   sauce
¼ teaspoon ground cardamom
½ cup water
cooked rice as an accompaniment

In a food processor or blender grind the walnuts to a paste. In a deep heavy skillet brown the chicken, patted dry, in the oil over moderately high heat and drain it on paper towels. Pour off all but 2 tablespoons of the fat and in the fat remaining in the skillet sauté the onion with the turmeric over moderately high heat until it is golden brown and stir in the walnut paste, the broth, the lemon juice, the tomato paste, the cranberry sauce, the cardamom, the water, and salt to taste. Bring the mixture to a boil, add the chicken, and cook the mixture, covered, over moderately low heat, stirring occasionally, for 20 minutes. Serve the chicken with the rice. Serves 2.

Braised Chicken Legs with Mushrooms and Peas

1½ pounds chicken legs (about 3), split
   into drumsticks and thighs
flour seasoned with salt and pepper for
   dredging the chicken
2 tablespoons olive oil
1 tablespoon unsalted butter
1 cup chopped onion
¼ teaspoon dried thyme, crumbled
¼ teaspoon dried rosemary, crumbled
⅓ cup chicken broth
⅓ cup dry white wine or dry vermouth
½ pound white mushrooms, sliced
1 cup frozen peas

Pat the chicken dry and dredge it in the seasoned flour, shaking off the excess. In a flame-proof casserole heat 1 tablespoon of the olive oil over moderately high heat until it is hot but not smoking, in it brown the chicken, and transfer the chicken with tongs to a plate. To the casserole add the butter, the onion, the thyme, the rosemary, and salt and pepper to taste and cook the mixture over moderately low heat, stirring, until the onion is softened. Return the chicken, skin sides up, to the casserole, add the broth and the wine, and bring the liquid to a boil. Braise the chicken, covered, in the middle of a preheated 450° F. oven for 15 minutes. While the chicken is braising, in a large heavy skillet heat the remaining 1 tablespoon olive oil over high heat until it is hot but not smoking and in it sauté the mushrooms until they are golden and the liquid they give off is evaporated. Season the mushrooms with salt and pepper and transfer them to the casserole. Add the peas, stirring, and bake the chicken, uncovered, in the 450° F. oven for 10 minutes. Transfer the chicken to a platter and spoon the peas and the mushrooms over it. Serves 2.

Chicken Thighs Provençale

4 chicken thighs with the skin and bone (about 1¼ pounds)
flour seasoned with salt and pepper for dredging the chicken
1 tablespoon olive oil
1 onion, chopped
1 small (½ pound) fennel bulb (sometimes called anise, available in most supermarkets), sliced thin plus the fennel leaves, chopped, for garnish
1 garlic clove, minced
1 tablespoon tomato paste
¼ teaspoon dried rosemary, crumbled
¼ teaspoon dried thyme, crumbled
¼ cup dry white wine or dry vermouth
¾ cup chicken broth
lemon juice to taste
buttered noodles as an accompaniment if desired

Pat the chicken dry with paper towels and dredge it in the seasoned flour, shaking off the excess. In a flameproof casserole heat the oil over moderately high heat until it is hot but not smoking, in it brown the chicken, and transfer the chicken with tongs to a plate. To the casserole add the onion, the sliced fennel, the garlic, the tomato paste, the rosemary, and the thyme and cook the mixture over moderate heat, stirring, for 3 minutes. Return the chicken, skin sides up, to the casserole, add the wine and the broth, and bring the liquid to a boil. Braise the chicken, covered, in a preheated 400° F. oven for 20 minutes, or until it is springy to the touch and just cooked through. Season the chicken with the lemon juice and salt and pepper, sprinkle it with the fennel leaves, and serve it over the noodles. Serves 2.

Garlic and Lemon Roast Chicken Thighs

2 garlic cloves, chopped
3 tablespoons fresh lemon juice
2 teaspoons Worcestershire sauce
½ teaspoon salt
1 pound chicken thighs
lemon wedges for garnish

In a blender purée the garlic with the lemon juice, the Worcestershire sauce, and the salt. In a resealable plastic bag combine the marinade with the chicken thighs and let the chicken marinate at room temperature for 15 minutes. Arrange the chicken, sprinkled with salt and pepper, on the rack of a foil-lined broiler pan, discarding the marinade. Roast the chicken in the middle of a preheated 425° F. oven for 25 to 35 minutes, or until it is springy to the touch and just cooked through. Serve the chicken with the lemon wedges. Serves 2.

Chicken Livers with Apple, Onion, and Calvados

1 onion, chopped
2 tablespoons unsalted butter
1 Granny Smith apple
¾ pound chicken livers, halved and trimmed
2 tablespoons all-purpose flour
1 tablespoon vegetable oil
¼ cup Calvados or apple brandy
5 tablespoons water
2 tablespoons minced fresh parsley leaves

In a heavy skillet cook the onion in 1 tablespoon of the butter over moderately low heat, stirring, until it is softened and transfer it to a plate. In the skillet sauté the apple, peeled and sliced thin, in the remaining tablespoon butter over moderately high heat, stirring until it is golden, and transfer it to the plate. In a bowl toss the chicken livers, patted dry, with the flour and salt and pepper to taste. Heat the oil in the skillet over moderately high heat until it is hot but not smoking, and in it sauté the chicken livers, turning them, for 3 minutes, or until they are just cooked through but still pink within. Add the onion, the apple, the Calvados, and the water and cook the mixture over moderate heat, stirring, for 2 minutes, or until the liquid is thickened. Stir in the parsley and salt and pepper to taste and divide the mixture between 2 heated plates. Serves 2.

Assorted Fowl

Roasted Rock Cornish Game Hen with Apple and Shallots

a 1½-pound Rock Cornish game hen, halved lengthwise and rinsed
1½ tablespoons vegetable oil
¼ cup Calvados or apple brandy
1 Granny Smith apple
8 medium shallots
½ teaspoon dried rosemary, crumbled fine
½ bay leaf
2 tablespoons cold unsalted butter, cut into bits
fresh lemon juice to taste
1 teaspoon minced scallion greens

Pat the hen dry. In a heavy ovenproof skillet heat the oil over moderately high heat until it is hot but not smoking and in it brown the hen, turning it. Transfer the hen to a dish, deglaze the skillet with the Calvados, scraping up the brown bits, and arrange the hen, skin side up, in the skillet. Peel, core, and cut the apple into ¼-inch wedges and scatter the apple wedges and the shallots around the hen. Sprinkle the hen with the rosemary and salt and pepper to taste, add the bay leaf, and put the skillet in a preheated 450° F. oven. Reduce the heat to 375° F. and roast the hen, basting it twice and adding a little water if necessary to keep ½ cup liquid in the skillet, for 30 minutes. Transfer the hen, the apple wedges, and the shallots to a platter. Discard the bay leaf, bring the liquid in the skillet to a boil, and boil it until it is reduced and thickened slightly. Whisk in the butter and the lemon juice and season the sauce with salt and pepper. Spoon the sauce over the hen and sprinkle the minced scallion greens over it. Serves 2.

Lemon Mustard Turkey Cutlets

four ¼-inch-thick turkey breast cutlets
1½ teaspoons freshly grated lemon zest
2 teaspoons Dijon-style mustard
2 tablespoons fresh lemon juice
3 tablespoons vegetable oil
½ cup fine dry bread crumbs
1 tablespoon minced fresh parsley leaves plus
  parsley sprigs for garnish if desired

In a dish large enough to hold the turkey cutlets in one layer whisk together the zest, the mustard, the lemon juice, 1 tablespoon of the oil, and salt and pepper to taste. Add the turkey, patted dry, turn it to coat it with the marinade, and let it marinate for 20 minutes.

In a shallow dish stir together the bread crumbs, the minced parsley, and salt and pepper to taste and dredge the turkey in the crumbs, shaking off the excess. In a very large heavy skillet heat the remaining 2 tablespoons oil over moderately high heat until it is hot but not smoking and in it sauté the cutlets for 30 seconds to 1 minute on each side, or until they are golden and cooked through. Divide the cutlets between 2 heated plates and garnish each serving with the parsley sprigs. Serves 2.

Turkey Slices with Lemon and Sage

2 tablespoons fresh lemon juice
½ teaspoon Dijon-style mustard
cayenne to taste
⅓ cup plus 1 tablespoon olive oil
2 tablespoons dried sage, crumbled
two 6-ounce skinless, boneless turkey breast
  slices, flattened ¼ inch thick between sheets
  of plastic wrap
lemon wedges and parsley sprigs for garnish

In a bowl combine the lemon juice, the mustard, the cayenne, and salt to taste, add ⅓ cup of the oil in a stream, whisking, and whisk the marinade until it is emulsified. Stir in the sage. Put the turkey in a shallow glass dish, pour the marinade over it, and let it marinate, covered, for 25 minutes.

In a large heavy skillet heat the remaining 1 tablespoon oil over moderately high heat until it is hot but not smoking and in it sauté the turkey, drained and patted dry, turning it once, for 2 minutes, or until it is just cooked through. Transfer the turkey to a platter and garnish it with the lemon wedges and the parsley. Serves 2.

Stir-Fried Turkey with Vegetables and Cashews

2 tablespoons vegetable oil
1 onion, sliced
1 green bell pepper, sliced thin
1 red bell pepper, sliced thin
1 cup sliced celery
½ teaspoon sugar
¾ cup chicken broth
¼ cup water
1 tablespoon soy sauce
1 teaspoon Oriental sesame oil
1 tablespoon cornstarch dissolved in
  2 tablespoons cold water
2 cups diced cooked turkey
cooked rice as an accompaniment
¼ cup chopped roasted cashews

In a large heavy skillet heat the vegetable oil until it is hot but not smoking and in it stir-fry the onion, the bell peppers, and the celery for 3 minutes, or until the vegetables are softened. Add the sugar, the broth, the water, the soy sauce, and the sesame oil and simmer the mixture, covered, for 3 minutes. Stir the cornstarch mixture, stir it into the vegetable mixture, and bring the liquid to a boil. Stir in the turkey and simmer the mixture until it is heated through. Serve the mixture over the rice and sprinkle it with the cashews. Serves 2.

Corn Waffles with Peppercorn Syrup

BREAKFAST, BRUNCH, AND CHEESE DISHES

W hether it is breakfast, brunch, or lunch—a quick bite on the run or a leisurely meal—here you will find appropriate fare that is universally loved. Omelets, frittatas, sausages, grits, waffles, pancakes, French toast, soufflés... all appear with extra-special touches that make them stand apart. Our French toast, for example, calls for a dab of blueberry jam to tuck into specially-made pockets, while our grilled Cheddar cheese sandwich adds pears and chutney for a surprisingly sweet and savory lunch.

If you are serving eggs, you will want to buy the freshest ones possible. Check the expiration date on the carton and then carefully shake one egg back and forth; if you can feel movement, the egg is old. When it comes time to add eggs to your batter, make sure they are still fresh, with firm, rounded yolks by cracking them, one by one, into a separate bowl before mixing them with other ingredients.

When you have overnight guests, you will want to serve breakfast without fuss. A few simple preparations the night before—such as cooking and chilling grits or chopping bell peppers or onions—can make a difference. These ingredients can be prepared and stored overnight. And, by setting up your coffeemaker with an automatic timer, you will be rewarded with an aromatic wake-up call.

Most of these recipes should be served piping hot. Have your plates warmed *before* you heat up the griddle. Squeeze some fresh juice for breakfast, or perhaps serve juice with a splash of champagne for brunch and lunch, and these little meals are complete.

Breakfast and Brunch Dishes
❦ ❦ ❦

Baked Eggs on Ham and Cheddar with Bell Pepper Sauce

◈4◈

2 slices of rye bread, toasted
2 ounces Cheddar, sliced thin
3 ounces cooked ham, chopped
2 large eggs
⅓ cup chicken broth
⅓ cup heavy cream
1 small red bell pepper, chopped

In a shallow baking pan top the toast slices with the cheese. Arrange the ham on the cheese slices, forming a nest, crack the eggs into the nests carefully, and season them with salt and pepper to taste. Bake the eggs in a preheated 350° F. oven for 15 minutes, or until the yolks are just set. While the eggs are baking, in a small heavy saucepan stir together the broth, the cream, and the bell pepper, bring the liquid to a boil, and boil it until it is reduced by half. Season the sauce with salt and pepper to taste. Arrange the toasts on 2 heated serving plates and spoon the sauce around them. Serves 2.

Eggs with Broccoli au Gratin

3 large eggs
1 cup broccoli flowerets
1 teaspoon minced onion
1 tablespoon unsalted butter
1 tablespoon all-purpose flour
¾ cup milk
white pepper to taste
½ cup freshly grated Parmesan

Put the eggs in a saucepan with enough cold water to cover them by 1 inch. Heat the water over high heat until large bubbles begin to rise from the bottom of the pan and reduce the heat to keep the water below the boiling point. Cook the eggs for 5 minutes, transfer them to a bowl of cold water, and let them cool. Remove the shells and chop the eggs.

In a steamer steam the broccoli for 3 minutes, or until it is crisp-tender, refresh it under cold water in a colander, and drain it, squeezing out any excess water gently.

In a saucepan cook the onion in the butter over moderately low heat, stirring, until it is softened, stir in the flour, and cook the *roux* over low heat, stirring, for 3 minutes. Add the milk in a stream, whisking vigorously until the mixture is thick and smooth. Add the white pepper and salt to taste and simmer the sauce for 10 to 15 minutes, or until it is very thick. Transfer the sauce to a bowl, add the eggs and the broccoli, and combine the mixture well. Divide the egg mixture between 2 buttered 5½-inch gratin dishes, sprinkle the tops with the Parmesan, and put the gratins under a preheated broiler about 2 to 3 inches from the heat until the tops are golden. Serves 2.

Bacon, Potato, and Gruyère Frittata

3 slices of bacon
1½ tablespoons olive oil
3 small red potatoes
4 large eggs
⅔ cup (about 3 ounces) grated Gruyère

In a 9-inch non-stick skillet cook the bacon until it is crisp and transfer it to paper towels to drain. Pour off all but ½ tablespoon of the fat in the pan, add 1 tablespoon of the olive oil, and in it sauté the potatoes, peeled, halved, and sliced thin, stirring, until they are tender and golden.

In a bowl whisk together the eggs, the bacon, crumbled, ⅓ cup of the Gruyère, and salt and pepper to taste, add the potatoes, and stir the mixture until it is combined well.

In the skillet heat the remaining ½ tablespoon olive oil over moderate heat until it is hot but not smoking, pour in the egg mixture, distributing the bacon and potatoes evenly, and cook the *frittata*, without stirring, for 8 to 10 minutes, or until the edge is set but the center is still soft. Sprinkle the remaining ⅓ cup Gruyère over the top. If the skillet handle is plastic, wrap it in a double thickness of foil. Broil the *frittata* under a preheated broiler about 4 inches from the heat for 2 to 3 minutes, or until the Gruyère is golden, and let it cool in the skillet for 5 minutes. Run a knife around the edge, slide the *frittata* onto a serving plate, and cut it into wedges. Serve the *frittata* warm or at room temperature. Serves 2.

Sausage and Grits Frittata

¾ cup water
3 tablespoons quick-cooking grits
¼ pound smoked *kielbasa,* sliced thin
½ cup finely chopped red bell pepper
1½ tablespoons olive oil
4 large eggs
4 scallions, sliced thin
½ cup finely grated sharp Cheddar
cayenne to taste

In a small heavy saucepan bring the water to a boil, add the grits and salt to taste, and cook the grits, covered, over low heat, stirring occasionally, for 5 minutes, or until it is very thick. Spoon the grits onto a sheet of plastic wrap, using the plastic wrap as a guide form them into a ½-inch-thick rectangle, and chill them, wrapped in the plastic wrap, for 15 minutes. Remove the plastic wrap and cut the grits into ½-inch dice.

In a 9-inch non-stick skillet cook the *kielbasa* and the bell pepper in 1 tablespoon of the oil over moderate heat, stirring, for 5 minutes. In a bowl whisk together the eggs, the scallions, the Cheddar, the cayenne, and salt to taste and stir in the *kielbasa* mixture and the diced grits, gently. In the skillet heat the remaining ½ tablespoon oil over moderate heat until it is hot but not smoking, pour in the egg mixture, and cook the *frittata*, without stirring, for 8 to 10 minutes, or until the edge is set but the center is still soft. If the skillet handle is plastic, wrap it in a double thickness of foil. Broil the *frittata* under a preheated broiler about 4 inches from the heat for 2 to 3 minutes, or until it is golden, and let it cool in the skillet for 5 minutes. Run a knife around the edge, slide the *frittata* onto a serving plate, and cut it into wedges. Serve the *frittata* warm or at room temperature. Serves 2.

Photo on page 16

Smoked Salmon, Sour Cream, and Scallion Omelet

1 tablespoon unsalted butter
4 large eggs, beaten lightly with 1 tablespoon
   cold water
¼ cup sour cream
2 ounces smoked salmon, chopped,
   or to taste
1 scallion including the green part, sliced

In an 8-inch non-stick skillet heat the butter over moderately high heat until the foam subsides and in it cook the eggs with salt and pepper to taste, undisturbed, for 5 seconds. Reduce the heat to moderate and cook the eggs, shaking the skillet and lifting the cooked portion to let the uncooked egg flow underneath it, until the omelet is just set but still soft and moist. Spread the omelet with the sour cream, and sprinkle it with the smoked salmon and the scallion. Fold the omelet over and slide it onto a plate. Halve the omelet and put each half on a heated plate. Serves 2.

Blueberry Vanilla French Toast

four 1-inch-thick diagonal slices of day-old
   French or Italian bread
2 tablespoons blueberry jam
2 large eggs, beaten lightly
½ cup milk
¼ cup heavy cream
2 tablespoons granulated sugar
¾ teaspoon vanilla
¼ teaspoon cinnamon
2 tablespoons unsalted butter
confectioners' sugar for sifting over the toast
maple syrup as an accompaniment

Cut through the bread slices horizontally to within ¼ inch of the crust, forming a pocket, in each pocket spread ½ tablespoon of the jam, and press the pockets closed. In a shallow bowl or pie plate large enough to hold the bread in one layer whisk together the eggs, the milk, the cream, the granulated sugar, the vanilla, the cinnamon, and a pinch of salt, add the filled bread, and let it soak, chilled, turning it once, for 25 minutes, or until it absorbs the egg mixture. In a heavy skillet heat the butter over moderate heat until the foam subsides and in it cook the soaked bread, turning it occasionally with a spatula, for 12 to 15 minutes, or until it is crisp and golden. Transfer

Cheddar Grits Rounds with Ham Hash

the toast with the spatula to heated plates, sift the confectioners' sugar over it, and serve it with the syrup. Serves 2.

Cheddar Grits Rounds with Ham Hash

2 cups water
6 tablespoons white hominy grits
(not quick-cooking)
½ pound red potatoes, scrubbed
½ cup grated sharp Cheddar
2 tablespoons unsalted butter
¼ pound cooked ham steak, cut into
¼-inch pieces
½ cup chopped onion
flour for dredging the grits rounds
1 large egg, beaten lightly
1 cup fine fresh bread crumbs seasoned with
salt and pepper
vegetable oil for frying the grits rounds
2 tablespoons finely chopped fresh
parsley leaves
ketchup as an accompaniment if desired

In a heavy saucepan bring the water to a boil, whisk in a pinch of salt and the grits, a little at a time, and simmer the mixture, covered, whisking occasionally, for 15 to 20 minutes, or until it is thickened. While the grits are cooking, cut the potatoes into ¼-inch pieces and in a saucepan of boiling salted water boil them for 2 minutes. Drain the potatoes in a sieve, refresh them under cold water, and pat them dry. Remove the grits mixture from the heat, stir in the Cheddar, and stir the mixture until the Cheddar is melted. Transfer the grits mixture to a metal bowl, set the bowl in a large pan of ice and cold water, and stir the grits mixture until it is cool. Spread the grits mixture in an 8-inch round cake pan, smoothing the top, and chill it, covered with plastic wrap, for 15 minutes. While the grits mixture is chilling, in a heavy ovenproof skillet heat the

butter over moderate heat until the foam subsides and in it cook the potatoes, the ham, and the onion, stirring, for 5 to 7 minutes, or until the potatoes are golden and tender. Keep the hash warm in a preheated 225° F. oven.

Run a thin knife around the edge of the grits mixture, turn the mixture out onto a sheet of plastic wrap, rapping the pan to release the mixture, and with a 2½-inch cutter cut out 6 rounds. Dredge the rounds in the flour, dip them in the egg, and coat them with the bread crumbs. In a large deep skillet heat ½ inch of the oil to 340° F., in it fry the rounds, turning them once, for 1 to 2 minutes, or until they are golden, and transfer them to paper towels to drain. Arrange the grits rounds on a heated platter, toss the hash with the parsley, and mound the hash in the center of the platter. Serve the grits rounds and the hash with the ketchup if desired. Serves 2.

Photo on page 118

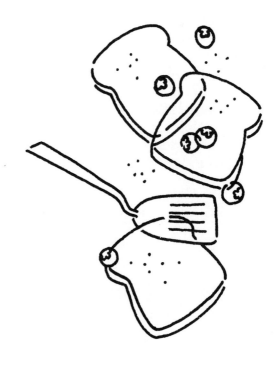

Pecan Pancakes

⅔ cup all-purpose flour
1 tablespoon granulated sugar
1 teaspoon double-acting baking powder
¾ teaspoon baking soda
⅓ cup plain yogurt
1 large egg, beaten lightly
1 tablespoon unsalted butter, melted and
    cooled, plus additional melted unsalted
    butter for brushing the griddle
½ teaspoon vanilla
½ cup milk
½ cup finely chopped lightly toasted pecans
maple syrup, heated, or sour cream,
    sweetened to taste with brown sugar,
    as an accompaniment

Into a bowl sift together the flour, the granulated sugar, the baking powder, the baking
soda, and a pinch of salt. In a large bowl whisk
together the yogurt, the egg, 1 tablespoon of
the butter, the vanilla, and the milk, stir the
mixture into the flour mixture, stirring until
the batter is just combined, and stir in the
pecans. Heat a griddle over moderately high
heat until it is hot but not smoking and brush
it with some of the additional melted butter.
Drop the batter by scant ¼ cups onto the griddle and cook the pancakes for 1 to 2 minutes,
or until the undersides are golden brown. Turn
the pancakes and cook them for 1 to 2 minutes more, or until the undersides are golden
brown. Serve the pecan pancakes with the
maple syrup or the sour cream. Makes about
eight 3-inch pancakes, serving 2.

Corn Waffles with Peppercorn Syrup

½ cup maple syrup
1½ teaspoons drained green peppercorns,
    crushed lightly, or ½ teaspoon freshly
    ground black pepper
½ cup all-purpose flour
½ cup yellow cornmeal
1 tablespoon sugar
2 teaspoons double-acting baking powder
¼ teaspoon salt
1 large egg
2 tablespoons unsalted butter, melted and
    cooled, plus additional unsalted butter
    as an accompaniment if desired
½ cup water
⅔ cup cooked fresh corn kernels or thawed
    frozen plus additional for garnish
vegetable oil for brushing the waffle iron
cooked breakfast sausage links as an
    accompaniment

In a small saucepan combine the syrup and the
peppercorns, bring the syrup just to a boil,
and let it stand off the heat while making the
waffles. In a bowl whisk together the flour, the
cornmeal, the sugar, the baking powder, and
the salt. In another bowl whisk together the
egg, the 2 tablespoons melted butter, the
water, and ⅔ cup of the corn, add the egg mixture to the flour mixture, and stir the batter
until it is just combined. Heat a waffle iron
until it is hot, brush it with the oil, and pour
half the batter onto it. Cook the waffle according to the manufacturer's instructions, transfer
it to a baking sheet, and keep it warm, uncovered, in a warm oven. Make another waffle
with the remaining batter in the same manner.
Serve the waffles on heated plates with the
syrup, the additional butter, the additional
corn, and the sausages. Serves 2.

Photo on page 114

Sausage and Red Bell Pepper Quiche

½ cup plus 2 tablespoons all-purpose flour
3 tablespoons cold unsalted butter,
   cut into bits
1 tablespoon cold vegetable shortening
½ teaspoon salt
¾ pound hot or sweet Italian sausages,
   casings discarded and the meat chopped
2 red bell peppers, minced (about 1¼ cups)
¼ cup grated Cheddar
2 tablespoons freshly grated Parmesan
2 large eggs
½ cup heavy cream
3 tablespoons milk

In a bowl blend together the flour, the butter, the shortening, and a pinch of the salt until the mixture resembles meal, add 1½ table-spoons of ice water, and toss the mixture until the water is incorporated, adding additional ice water if necessary to form the dough into a ball. Pat the dough into a 7½-inch tart pan with a removable rim and bake the shell in the bottom third of a preheated 425° F. oven for 7 minutes, or until it is just golden.

    While the shell is baking, in a large skillet cook the sausage with the bell peppers, cov-ered, over moderately high heat, stirring and breaking up any lumps, for 7 minutes, or until the sausage is no longer pink and the bell pep-pers are soft, and drain the mixture, discarding the excess fat. Transfer the mixture to a bowl, stir in the remaining salt, the Cheddar, and the Parmesan, and spread the mixture in the bot-tom of the shell. In a bowl whisk together the eggs, the cream, and the milk, pour the egg mixture over the sausage mixture, and bake the quiche on a baking sheet in the middle of a preheated 425° F. oven for 15 minutes. Reduce the temperature to 350° F. and bake the quiche for 10 minutes more. Serves 2.

Photo on this page

Sausage and Red Bell Pepper Quiche

Cheese Dishes

Fried Feta with Orégano Vinaigrette

1 teaspoon white-wine vinegar
½ teaspoon dried orégano, crumbled
1½ tablespoons olive oil
¼ pound Feta, cut into four ½-inch-thick slices
flour for dredging the Feta
1 large egg, beaten well
⅔ cup fine fresh bread crumbs
1½ tablespoons unsalted butter

In a small bowl whisk together the vinegar, the orégano, and pepper to taste and whisk in the oil. Dredge the Feta slices in the flour, brushing off any excess carefully, dip them in the egg, and roll them in the bread crumbs, patting the crumbs gently onto the sides. In a heavy skillet heat the butter over moderate heat until the foam subsides, in it cook the Feta, turning it once, for 3 to 5 minutes, or until it is golden, and divide the cheese between 2 heated serving plates. Whisk the vinaigrette and drizzle it over the Feta. Serves 2 as a first course or a light luncheon entrée.

Welsh Rabbit with Canadian Bacon and Scallion

1½ cups coarsely grated extra-sharp Cheddar
2 tablespoons beer or medium-dry Sherry
1 teaspoon Worcestershire sauce, or to taste
½ teaspoon dry mustard
a pinch of cayenne
2 slices of Canadian bacon
½ tablespoon unsalted butter
1 English muffin, halved, toasted, and buttered lightly
1½ tablespoons chopped scallion

In a bowl toss together the Cheddar, the beer, the Worcestershire sauce, the mustard, the cayenne, and salt and pepper. In a small skillet sauté the Canadian bacon in the butter over moderately high heat until the edges are crisp. Arrange the English muffin halves in a gratin dish or shallow baking dish just large enough to hold them in 1 layer, top each half with a slice of the bacon, half the Cheddar mixture, and half the scallion, and put the dish under a preheated broiler about 4 inches from the heat for 3 to 4 minutes, or until the cheese is melted and browned lightly. Serves 2.

Fried Mozzarella with Sun-Dried Tomato Vinaigrette and Basil

½ cup fine dry bread crumbs
flour for dredging the mozzarella
1 large egg
an 8-ounce package mozzarella, sliced horizontally into four ¼-inch-thick slices
¼ cup drained sun-dried tomatoes (packed in oil)
¼ cup olive oil
2 teaspoons balsamic vinegar
1 plum tomato, chopped
⅓ cup water
2 tablespoons minced fresh basil leaves plus additional for garnish if desired

In a small shallow bowl stir together the bread crumbs and salt and pepper to taste. Have ready in 2 separate bowls the flour and the egg, beaten lightly. Working with 1 mozzarella slice at a time, dredge the slices in the flour, shaking off the excess, dip them in the egg, letting the excess drip off, and coat them with the crumb mixture, patting the crumbs gently onto the sides and edges. Line a plate with wax paper and on it chill the slices in one layer for 15 minutes. While the mozzarella is chilling, in a blender blend the sun-dried tomatoes, 2 tablespoons of the oil, the vinegar, the plum tomato, the water, and salt and pepper to taste until the mixture is smooth. Transfer the sauce to a bowl, stir in 2 tablespoons of the basil, and divide the sauce between 2 plates. In a large, heavy non-stick skillet heat the remaining 2 tablespoons oil over moderately high heat until it is hot but not smoking and in it sauté the mozzarella slices, turning them once, for 1 to 1½ minutes on each side, or until they are golden. Divide the slices between the plates and garnish them with the additional basil. Serves 2 as a luncheon entrée.

Saga Blue Soufflés with Port Sauce

1 tablespoon fine dry bread crumbs
1 tablespoon freshly grated Parmesan
6 ounces Saga blue or Bavarian blue cheese,
  rind discarded, at room temperature
3 large eggs, separated
a pinch of cream of tartar

For the sauce
½ cup Ruby Port
2 tablespoons minced shallot
1½ cups chicken broth combined with
  1 envelope of unflavored gelatin
2 tablespoons red currant jelly
1 teaspoon Dijon-style mustard
1 tablespoon unsalted butter, softened

For the garnish
2 small clusters of green grapes
2 sprigs of watercress

In a small bowl combine the bread crumbs and the Parmesan. Coat the bottom and sides of 2 buttered 1-cup soufflé dishes with the crumb mixture, shaking out the excess, and chill the dishes. In a food processor blend the Saga blue until it is smooth and add the egg yolks. Blend the mixture well and transfer it to a bowl. In another bowl with an electric mixer beat the egg whites with a pinch of salt until they are frothy, add the cream of tartar, and beat the whites until they just hold stiff peaks. Stir one third of the whites into the cheese

mixture and fold in the remaining whites gently. Spoon the soufflé mixture into the dishes and smooth the tops gently. Put the soufflés in a baking pan, add enough hot water to the pan to come halfway up the sides of the soufflé dishes, and bake the soufflés in a preheated 375° F. oven for 20 to 25 minutes, or until they are puffed and golden brown.

Make the sauce while the soufflés are baking: In a saucepan combine the Port and the shallot, bring the Port to a boil, and boil it until it is reduced to about 2 tablespoons. Add the broth mixture and boil the liquid until it is reduced to about ⅔ cup. Add the jelly and cook the mixture over moderately low heat, stirring, until the jelly is melted. Whisk in the mustard, the butter, and salt and pepper to taste and keep the sauce warm.

Let the soufflés stand for 2 minutes, lift them gently from the dishes, and transfer them to heated plates. Pour the sauce around the soufflés and garnish the soufflés with the grapes and the watercress. Serves 2 as a luncheon entrée.

Grilled Cheddar, Pear, and Chutney Sandwiches

2 tablespoons bottled mango chutney,
  minced
4 slices of homemade-type whole-wheat
  bread
4 ounces sharp Cheddar, sliced thin
½ small, firm-ripe pear, sliced thin
1½ tablespoons unsalted butter, melted

Spread the chutney on 2 of the bread slices, divide half the Cheddar between the chutney-topped slices, and divide the pear between them. Top each sandwich with the remaining Cheddar and the remaining bread slices. Brush both sides of the sandwiches with the butter. In a heavy skillet cook the sandwiches over moderate heat, for 2 to 3 minutes on each side, or until they are golden. Serves 2.

Fusilli with Carrots, Peas, and Mint

PASTA

F

ettuccine, fusilli, penne, tortellini… the cornucopia of pasta shapes is fantastic! Here we have chosen a few of our favorites and combined them with simple, innovative sauces. Delicious, economical, *and* healthful, pasta is the ideal fast food.

There are two types of pasta: fresh and dried. The fresh variety is usually paired with light tomato sauces and cream-based sauces that adhere to it best. Fresh pasta can be found in pasta shops, and it is also available in most supermarkets. Dried pasta is made with a sturdier dough and it is more versatile. You can always feel free to substitute and experiment with different pasta shapes.

Cooking pasta is simple with these easy steps: Use a large, thin metal pot filled with lots of water (about 3 quarts to ½ pound of pasta) so the pasta has plenty of room to move about and will not stick together. Salt the boiling water liberally (1 teaspoon salt per 1 quart of water), then add the pasta and cook until it is *al dente* ("to the tooth"), which means tender but firm. Cooking times will vary according to the type and shape of pasta. The best way to test if pasta is done is to taste it. Also, cooked pasta should never be rinsed unless it is to be served cold, as in some pasta salads and Oriental noodle dishes.

Finally, you will notice that many of our recipes call for Parmesan cheese as a finishing touch. This slighty salty, sharp-tasting cheese quickly looses its flavor after grating, so buy a wedge and grate it fresh as needed. The cheese keeps for months in the bottom of the refrigerator, wrapped in foil.

Fettuccine with Basil Cream Sauce

½ cup thinly sliced shallot
1½ tablespoons unsalted butter
¾ cup heavy cream
1 tablespoon Pernod or other anise-flavored
    liqueur if desired
3 ounces dried spinach fettuccine
¼ cup minced fresh basil leaves plus small
    whole leaves for garnish

In a small heavy skillet cook the shallot in the butter over moderate heat, stirring occasionally, until the shallot is golden, stir in the cream, the Pernod, and salt to taste, and cook the mixture, stirring occasionally, for 5 minutes, or until the sauce is thickened. While the sauce is cooking, in a large saucepan of boiling salted water cook the fettuccine for 8 to 10 minutes, or until it is *al dente*, and drain it well. In a bowl toss the fettuccine with the sauce and the minced basil, divide it between 2 plates, and garnish it with the small basil leaves. Serves 2 as a first course.

Fettuccine with Cherry Tomatoes, Goat Cheese, and Herbs

½ pound fettuccine
¼ cup olive oil
1 tablespoon minced garlic
2 tablespoons minced fresh parsley leaves,
    or to taste, plus, if desired, parsley sprigs
    for garnish
2 tablespoons minced fresh mint leaves,
    or to taste
1 to 1½ cups cherry tomatoes, quartered
3 ounces mild goat cheese such as
    Montrachet, crumbled (about ¾ cup)

In a kettle of boiling salted water cook the fettuccine for 8 to 10 minutes, or until it is *al dente*. While the fettuccine is cooking, in a small saucepan heat the oil and the garlic over

moderately low heat just until the mixture is hot and remove the pan from the heat. Drain the fettuccine well and in a bowl toss it with the oil mixture, the minced parsley, the mint, the tomatoes, the goat cheese, and salt and pepper to taste. Divide the pasta between 2 plates and garnish it with the parsley sprigs. Serves 2.

Photo on page 127

Fusilli with Broccoli and Garlic

2 large garlic cloves, minced
¼ teaspoon dried hot red pepper flakes
3 tablespoons olive oil
¾ pound broccoli, cut into small flowerets and
    the stems sliced thin
½ cup water
½ pound *fusilli* (spiral-shaped pasta)
freshly grated Parmesan as an accompani-
    ment if desired

In a large heavy skillet cook the garlic and the red pepper flakes in the olive oil over moderate heat, stirring, until the garlic is golden, add the broccoli, and cook it, stirring, for 1 minute, or until it is a brighter green. Add the water and steam the broccoli, covered, over moderately high heat for 5 minutes, or until it is tender.

While the broccoli is steaming, stir the *fusilli* into a kettle of boiling salted water and cook it for 8 to 10 minutes, or until it is *al dente*. Drain the *fusilli* and add it to the broccoli mixture. Heat the mixture over moderate heat, stirring, until it is combined well and heated through, season it with salt and pepper, and divide it between 2 heated plates. Serve the *fusilli* with the Parmesan. Serves 2.

Fusilli with Carrots, Peas, and Mint

¾ cup fresh bread crumbs
2 tablespoons olive oil
½ cup finely chopped shallot
1 cup cooked fresh or thawed frozen peas
¾ cup chicken broth
1¼ cups coarsely grated (preferably in a food
processor) carrots
¼ cup heavy cream
½ pound *fusilli* (spiral-shaped pasta)
or fettuccine
¼ cup minced fresh mint leaves

In a skillet cook the bread crumbs in 1 tablespoon of the oil over moderate heat, stirring, until they are golden and crisp and transfer them to a small bowl. In the skillet cook the shallot in the remaining 1 tablespoon oil over moderately low heat, stirring, until it is softened, add the peas and the broth, and simmer the mixture, stirring, for 3 minutes. Stir in the carrots, simmer the mixture, stirring, for 2 minutes, or until the carrots are just tender, and stir in the cream and salt and pepper to taste. Simmer the mixture until the liquid is reduced by about one fourth, remove the sauce from the heat, and keep it warm.

In a kettle of boiling salted water cook the *fusilli* for 8 to 10 minutes, or until it is *al dente*, drain it well, and in a bowl toss it with the sauce, half of the bread crumbs, and the mint. Divide the *fusilli* between 2 soup bowls and top it with the remaining bread crumbs. Serves 2.

Photo on page 124

Fettuccine with Cherry Tomatoes, Goat Cheese, and Herbs

Fusilli with Corn and Uncooked Tomato Sauce

1½ tablespoons red-wine vinegar
3 tablespoons olive oil, or to taste
½ cup cooked corn kernels, cut from
   1 ear of corn
1 pound tomatoes, seeded and chopped
¼ cup thinly sliced scallion
½ pound *fusilli* or other spiral-shaped pasta

In a large bowl whisk together the vinegar, the oil, and salt and pepper to taste and stir in the corn, the tomatoes, and the scallion. In a kettle of boiling salted water cook the *fusilli* for 8 to 10 minutes, or until it is *al dente*, and drain it well. Transfer the *fusilli* to the bowl and toss the mixture well. Serves 2.

Linguine with Asparagus and Prosciutto

1 onion, chopped fine
1½ teaspoons minced garlic
⅛ teaspoon dried thyme, crumbled
2 tablespoons olive oil
1 tablespoon unsalted butter
¾ pound asparagus, trimmed, peeled, and
   sliced thin diagonally
2 ounces prosciutto, chopped
½ pound dried *linguine*
1 tablespoon water
1 tablespoon fresh lemon juice, or to taste
2 tablespoons freshly grated Parmesan

In a heavy skillet cook the onion, the garlic, and the thyme in the oil and the butter over moderate heat, stirring, until the onion is soft. Add the asparagus and the prosciutto and cook the mixture over moderate heat, stirring, for 2 minutes.

   While the sauce is cooking, in a kettle of boiling salted water cook the *linguine* for 8 to 10 minutes, or until it is *al dente*, and drain it.

   Remove the sauce from the heat, add the water, the lemon juice, the *linguine*, the Parmesan, and salt and pepper to taste, and toss the mixture well. Serves 2.

Linguine with Broccoli Rabe and Lemon

1 bunch (about 1 pound) broccoli rabe
2 slices of bacon, cut into julienne strips
½ cup thinly sliced red onion
2 garlic cloves, minced
⅓ cup minced fresh parsley leaves
1 tablespoon fresh lemon juice, or to taste
¼ teaspoon freshly grated lemon zest
¼ teaspoon dried hot red pepper flakes
½ pound *linguine*

Trim and discard any yellow or coarse leaves and the tough stem ends from the broccoli rabe and chop the broccoli rabe coarse. Wash the broccoli rabe in a colander and drain it. In a large heavy skillet cook the bacon over moderate heat, stirring, until it is crisp and transfer it with a slotted spoon to paper towels to drain. Pour off all but 2 tablespoons of the fat and in the fat remaining in the skillet cook the onion and the garlic over moderately low heat, stirring, until the onion is softened. Remove the skillet from the heat and stir in the parsley, the lemon juice, the zest, the red pepper flakes, and salt to taste.

   In a kettle of boiling salted water cook the *linguine* for 8 to 10 minutes, or until it is *al dente*, adding the broccoli rabe 1 minute before the pasta is done. Drain the *linguine* mixture well and transfer it to the skillet. Toss the *linguine* mixture with the onion mixture until it is combined well and sprinkle it with the bacon. Serves 2.

Photo on page 129

Linguine with Shrimp and Saffron Sauce

⅛ teaspoon crumbled saffron threads
½ cup dry white wine or dry vermouth
⅓ pound dried *linguine*
2 teaspoons turmeric
2 tablespoons vegetable oil
½ pound medium shrimp (about 14), shelled, leaving the tail intact, deveined, rinsed, and patted dry
1 teaspoon minced garlic
¼ cup minced shallot
½ cup chicken broth
¾ cup heavy cream
3 carrots, cut into ribbonlike strands with a vegetable peeler, discarding the cores
½ cup thawed frozen green peas
the green part of 4 scallions, sliced very thin lengthwise

In a small bowl let the saffron soak in the wine for 5 minutes. In a kettle of boiling salted water cook the *linguine* with the turmeric for 8 to 10 minutes, or until it is *al dente*. While the *linguine* is cooking, in a large skillet heat the oil over moderate heat until it is hot but not smoking and in it cook the shrimp, stirring, for 1 minute. Add the garlic and salt and pepper to taste, cook the mixture, stirring, until the shrimp just turn pink, and transfer the shrimp with tongs to a plate. Add the shallot and the saffron mixture to the skillet and boil the mixture until almost all the liquid is evaporated. Add the broth, the cream, and the carrots and boil the mixture until the liquid is reduced by half. Add the peas, the scallion greens, the *linguine*, drained well, the shrimp and any juices that have accumulated on the plate, and salt and pepper to taste and simmer the mixture until it is just heated through. Serves 2.

Photo on page 18

Linguine with Broccoli Rabe and Lemon

Linguine with Clam and Sun-Dried Tomato Sauce

1 large onion, minced
2 garlic cloves, minced
2 tablespoons olive oil
1 tablespoon unsalted butter
¾ cup dry white wine or dry vermouth
¾ cup water
18 small hard-shelled clams, scrubbed well
¼ cup minced fresh parsley leaves plus parsley
    sprigs for garnish
¼ teaspoon dried thyme, crumbled
¼ cup drained sun-dried tomatoes (packed
    in oil), chopped
¼ pound dried *linguine*
freshly grated Parmesan as an
    accompaniment

In a skillet cook the onion and the garlic in the oil and the butter over moderately low heat, stirring occasionally, until the vegetables are softened. While the vegetables are cooking, in a large saucepan bring the wine and the water to a boil, add the clams, and steam them, covered, for 5 minutes, or until they begin to open. As the clams open, transfer them with tongs to a bowl and continue to steam the unopened clams, shaking the pan and transferring them as they open, for up to 10 minutes more. (Discard any remaining unopened clams.) Reserve 6 clams in their shells and 1 cup of the cooking liquid. Remove the remaining 12 clams from their shells and chop them coarse. Whisk the reserved cooking liquid into the skillet. Bring the mixture to a boil, stir in the minced parsley, the thyme, the sun-dried tomatoes, and salt and pepper to taste, and simmer the mixture, stirring occasionally, for 5 minutes. While the mixture is cooking, in a large saucepan of boiling salted water cook the *linguine* for 8 to 10 minutes, or until it is *al dente*, drain it well, and divide it between 2 heated bowls. Stir the chopped clams into the skillet and cook the sauce, stirring, until the

clams are just heated through. Spoon the sauce over the *linguine*, arrange the reserved clams on top, and garnish the *linguine* with the parsley sprigs. Serve the *linguine* with the Parmesan. Serves 2.

Macaroni and Cheese with Bell Pepper and Pepperoni

1 cup chopped red bell pepper
½ cup chopped sliced pepperoni
    (about 2 ounces)
2 tablespoons vegetable oil
2 tablespoons all-purpose flour
1 cup milk
2 ounces sharp Cheddar, grated (about ½ cup)
¾ cup dried elbow macaroni

In a large saucepan cook the bell pepper and the pepperoni in the oil over moderately high heat, stirring occasionally, for 5 minutes. Reduce the heat to low, add the flour, and cook the mixture, stirring, for 3 minutes. Stir in the milk, bring the mixture to a boil, stirring, and simmer it, stirring occasionally, for 5 minutes. Add the Cheddar and cook the mixture over moderately low heat, stirring, until the cheese is melted. While the sauce is cooking, in a large saucepan of boiling salted water cook the macaroni for 10 to 12 minutes, or until it is *al dente*, and drain it. Add the macaroni to the sauce with salt and pepper to taste and stir the mixture until it is combined well. Transfer the macaroni and cheese to a shallow flameproof baking dish and broil it under a preheated broiler about 4 inches from the heat for 3 to 4 minutes, or until the top is browned lightly and the mixture is heated through. Serves 2.

Penne with Italian Sausage and Zucchini

1 onion, chopped
1 tablespoon vegetable oil
two 3-ounce uncooked hot or sweet Italian
    sausages, casings discarded
a 14- to 16-ounce can tomatoes, drained,
    reserving ½ cup of the juice, and chopped
½ cup water
1 garlic clove, minced
1 zucchini, halved lengthwise and cut cross-
    wise into ¼-inch slices
¼ cup minced fresh parsley leaves
½ pound *penne* (quill-shaped pasta)
freshly grated Parmesan as an accompani-
    ment if desired

In a large heavy skillet cook the onion in the oil over moderately low heat, stirring, until it is softened. Add the sausage and cook the mixture over moderate heat, stirring and breaking up the lumps, until the meat is no longer pink. Stir in the tomatoes with the ½ cup juice, the water, the garlic, and salt and pepper to taste, bring the liquid to a boil, and simmer the mixture, stirring occasionally, for 10 minutes. Stir in the zucchini and the parsley and simmer the mixture for 10 to 15 minutes, or until the zucchini is crisp-tender. While the sauce is cooking, in a kettle of boiling salted water cook the *penne* for 12 to 15 minutes, or until it is *al dente*, drain it well, and transfer it to a heated bowl. Toss the *penne* with the sauce and serve it with the Parmesan. Serves 2.

Penne with Tomato Cream Sauce

a 14- to 16-ounce can Italian plum tomatoes
    including the juice
½ cup heavy cream
1 garlic clove, minced
¾ teaspoon dried tarragon, crumbled
½ pound *penne* (quill-shaped pasta)
3 tablespoons freshly grated Parmesan

In a heavy saucepan combine the tomatoes with the juice, the cream, the garlic, the tarragon, and salt to taste, bring the liquid to a boil, breaking up the tomatoes, and simmer the mixture, stirring occasionally, for 25 to 30 minutes, or until the sauce is thickened.

In a kettle of boiling salted water boil the *penne* for 12 to 15 minutes, or until it is *al dente*, drain it well, and in the pan toss it with the tomato sauce. Serve the *penne* sprinkled with the Parmesan. Serves 2.

Won Ton Ravioli with Eggplant Filling

For the filling
1 cup peeled and finely chopped eggplant
4 teaspoons minced onion
2½ teaspoons minced green bell pepper
¼ teaspoon minced garlic
a pinch of dried orégano, crumbled
2 tablespoons olive oil
½ cup water
4½ teaspoons whole-milk ricotta
1 tablespoon freshly grated Parmesan
1 tablespoon minced fresh parsley leaves
1 large egg yolk, beaten lightly

**8 won ton wrappers (thawed if frozen),
    covered with a dampened
    kitchen towel**
4 tablespoons freshly grated Parmesan
2 tablespoons unsalted butter, melted
1 tablespoon minced fresh parsley leaves

Make the filling: In a skillet sauté the eggplant, the onion, the bell pepper, the garlic, and the orégano in the olive oil over moderately high heat, stirring, for 1 minute, add the water, and cook the mixture, covered, for 5 minutes, or until the liquid is evaporated. Transfer the mixture to a metal bowl, let it cool slightly, and stir in the ricotta, the Parmesan, the parsley, the egg yolk, and salt and pepper to taste.

Put 1 won ton wrapper on a clean, dry work surface with a corner facing you and mound 2 rounded teaspoons of the filling in the center of it. Moisten the edges of the wrapper with a little water, fold the corner facing you over the filling to form a triangle, and pinch the edges together, sealing them well. Make won ton ravioli in the same manner with the remaining wrappers and filling.

In a kettle of boiling salted water cook the ravioli for 8 minutes, drain them in a colander, and rinse them briefly under cold water. Arrange the ravioli on a heated platter, sprin-

kle them with the Parmesan, and drizzle them with the butter. Sprinkle the ravioli with the parsley. Serves 2 as a first course or a light luncheon entrée.

Cheese Ravioli with Sun-Dried Tomato and Basil Pesto

**⅓ cup drained sun-dried tomatoes
    (packed in oil)**
**¼ cup chopped fresh basil leaves, plus whole
    basil leaves for garnish if desired**
**1 garlic clove, minced and mashed to a paste
    with ¼ teaspoon salt**
¼ cup olive oil
2 tablespoons freshly grated Parmesan
¾ pound fresh or frozen cheese ravioli

In a blender or food processor grind together the sun-dried tomatoes and the chopped basil, add the garlic paste, the oil, and the Parmesan, and blend the mixture until it is combined. In a kettle of boiling salted water boil the ravioli gently for 10 to 20 minutes, or until they are tender. Reserve ¼ cup of the cooking liquid and drain the ravioli. Add the reserved cooking liquid to the tomato mixture and blend the pesto until it is smooth. In a bowl toss the ravioli with the *pesto*, divide them between 2 heated plates, and garnish each serving with the basil leaves. Serves 2.

Rigatoni with Hot Sausage, Fennel, and Artichokes

serves 4

½ pound hot Italian sausage (about 3),
    casings discarded
1 tablespoon olive oil
1 onion, chopped
1 large garlic clove, minced
1 red bell pepper, chopped
1 small fennel bulb (sometimes called anise,
    available in most supermarkets), trimmed
    and sliced thin (about 2 cups), plus fennel
    sprigs, chopped
⅓ cup dry white wine or dry vermouth
½ cup chicken broth
¼ cup heavy cream
½ cup drained marinated artichoke hearts,
    chopped coarse
½ pound rigatoni or other tubular pasta
¼ cup minced scallion
freshly grated Parmesan to taste

In a heavy skillet cook the sausage over moderate heat, stirring and breaking up any lumps, until it is cooked through, transfer it with a slotted spoon to paper towels to drain, and pour off all but 1 tablespoon of the fat. Add the oil to the skillet and in it cook the onion and the garlic over moderately low heat, stirring, until the onion is softened. Add the bell pepper and the sliced fennel and cook the mixture over moderate heat, stirring occasionally, for 5 minutes, or until the vegetables are softened. Add the wine and the broth, bring the liquid to a boil, and simmer the mixture, covered, for 5 minutes. Add the cream and the artichoke hearts and boil the mixture until the liquid is thickened slightly and reduced by about one third. Stir in the sausage and salt and pepper to taste. Keep the sauce warm.

In a kettle of boiling salted water cook the rigatoni for 12 minutes, or until it is *al dente*, and drain it well. In a bowl toss the sauce with the rigatoni, the scallion, the fennel sprigs, and the Parmesan. Serves 2 generously.

Spaghetti with Spicy Calamari, Garlic, and Tomato

serves 4

½ pound spaghetti
3 tablespoons olive oil
½ pound cleaned calamari, the body sacs cut
    into ¼-inch rings and the tentacles chopped
3 large garlic cloves, sliced thin lengthwise
3 tablespoons finely chopped fresh parsley
    leaves
⅓ cup canned tomato purée
¼ teaspoon dried hot red pepper flakes

In a kettle of boiling salted water cook the spaghetti for 10 minutes, or until it is *al dente*. While the spaghetti is cooking, in a large heavy skillet heat 1 tablespoon of the olive oil over moderately high heat until it is hot but not smoking, pat the calamari dry with paper towels, and sauté it, stirring, for 30 seconds, or until it is just firm and white. Transfer the calamari with a slotted spoon to a bowl. Add the remaining 2 tablespoons oil to the skillet and cook the garlic in the oil over moderately low heat, stirring, until it is golden, being careful not to let it get too brown. Stir in the parsley, the tomato purée, the red pepper flakes, and salt and pepper to taste and cook the sauce, stirring, for 1 minute. Keep the sauce warm.

Drain the spaghetti, reserving about ⅓ cup of the cooking water. Add the spaghetti to the sauce with the calamari and ¼ cup of the reserved cooking water and toss the spaghetti mixture over low heat for 1 minute, adding the remaining reserved cooking water if desired. Divide the spaghetti mixture between 2 heated plates and season it with pepper to taste. Serves 2.

Oriental Spaghetti with Shredded Vegetables and Spicy Peanut Sauce

For the sauce
¼ cup smooth peanut butter
1 tablespoon soy sauce
1 tablespoon rice vinegar or white-wine vinegar
1 small garlic clove, chopped
cayenne to taste
¼ teaspoon sugar
¼ cup hot water

1 carrot, cut into 3-inch pieces and each piece cut lengthwise into ⅛-inch shreds
¼ pound snow peas, trimmed and cut lengthwise into ⅛-inch shreds
6 ounces spaghetti
2 scallions, cut into 3-inch pieces and each piece cut lengthwise into ⅛-inch shreds

Make the sauce: In a blender blend the peanut butter, the soy sauce, the vinegar, the garlic, the cayenne, the sugar, and the water until the sauce is smooth.

In a kettle of boiling salted water boil the carrots for 2 minutes and with a slotted spoon transfer them to a bowl of ice water to stop the cooking. In the kettle boil the snow peas for 15 seconds and with the slotted spoon transfer them to the bowl of ice water to stop the cooking. In the kettle boil the spaghetti for 10 minutes, or until it is just tender, drain it in a colander, and rinse it briefly under cold water. Drain the spaghetti well, transfer it to a bowl, and toss it with the sauce, the carrots and the snow peas, drained, the scallions, and salt and pepper to taste. Serve the pasta at room temperature. Serves 2.

Spaghettini with Cauliflower, Prosciutto, and Chives

2 cups small cauliflower flowerets
½ pound spaghettini
2 tablespoons unsalted butter
½ cup heavy cream
2 ounces prosciutto, chopped
½ cup freshly grated Parmesan
2 tablespoons minced fresh chives

In a kettle of boiling salted water cook the cauliflower for 3 minutes, or until it is tender, and with a slotted spoon transfer it to a bowl. In the kettle cook the spaghettini for 8 to 10 minutes, or until it is *al dente*, and drain it, reserving ⅓ cup of the cooking water. Return the spaghettini to the kettle with the cauliflower and the reserved cooking water, add the butter and the cream, and bring the liquid to a simmer over moderate heat, stirring. Stir in the prosciutto, the Parmesan, and the chives, cook the mixture, stirring, until it is very hot, and season it with salt and pepper. Serves 2.

Spätzle with Caraway Scallion Sauce

For the sauce
¼ cup finely chopped scallion
1 small garlic clove, minced
1 tablespoon unsalted butter
½ teaspoon caraway seeds
1 teaspoon all-purpose flour
⅓ cup chicken broth
½ teaspoon fresh lemon juice, or to taste

For the Spätzle
1 large egg
¼ cup milk
1 tablespoon water
½ teaspoon salt
¾ cup all-purpose flour

1 tablespoon minced fresh parsley leaves

Make the sauce: In a small saucepan cook the scallion and the garlic in the butter over moder-ately low heat, stirring, until they are softened, stir in the caraway seeds and the flour, and cook the *roux*, stirring, for 3 minutes. Add the broth, the lemon juice, and salt and pepper to taste, simmer the sauce, stirring, for 2 minutes, and keep it warm, covered.

Make the *Spätzle*: In a small bowl whisk together the egg, the milk, the water, and the salt, add the flour, and beat the mixture with a wooden spoon until it is just smooth. Transfer the batter to a pastry bag fitted with a ⅜-inch plain tip. In a large deep skillet bring 2 inches salted water to a bare simmer. Holding the pastry bag in one hand with the tip resting just over the rim of the skillet and working quickly, cut off ¼-inch segments of the batter from the pastry tip with a knife, letting the batter drop into the water. When all the batter is used, cook the *Spätzle* for 5 minutes, or until it is *al dente*, drain it in a sieve, and rinse it quickly under cold water.

Add the *Spätzle* to the sauce, cook the mixture over moderate heat, stirring, until it is heated through, and stir in the parsley. Serves 2.

135

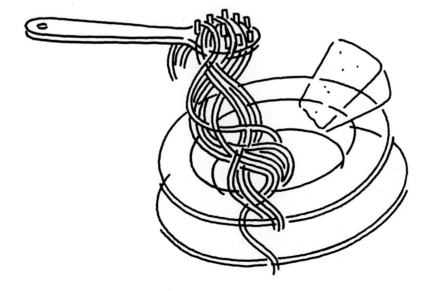

Lemon Broccoli Risotto

T he Western world is finally coming to realize what the East has known for centuries—grains are delicious and good for us. They add flavor and texture to any meal, and they are high in fiber.

Grain is the seed-bearing fruit of wheat, corn, or rice plants. Each kernel has a fibrous outer coat, or "bran," an oil-rich inner seed, and an innermost endosperm filled with starch and protein. Most grains are processed to remove tough husks, to make cooking quicker, or to render them easier to chew. Whole grains, however, leave the bran intact and are the most nutritious.

We urge you to try a sampling of our recipes to become familiar with the different tastes of various grains. There is the familiar, hearty flavor of cornmeal, the earthy savor of barley and kasha, and the nutlike taste of bulgur. And, although it is technically a pasta, we have also included couscous here for its grainlike light, fluffy texture. Naturally, there are several rice dishes, too. Converted rice is treated with steam-pressure which forces all nutrients from the outer bran into the endosperm; it is firm when cooked. Feel free to use either converted rice or rice that has not been converted, unless otherwise specified in our recipes.

Supermarkets are carrying more and more grains these days, but in some areas you may need to rely on your natural-foods shop for rarer varieties, such as kasha and bulgur. At home keep grains in airtight containers in a cool, dry, dark place. When cooking grains, just remember that they expand as they cook (barley quadruples), so choose your pan carefully. Two of our couscous recipes call for timbale molds, and these can be found at cookware shops; alternatively, use custard cups.

Bulgur Pilaf with Cashews and Spices

1 small onion
¼ teaspoon ground coriander seed
¼ teaspoon cinnamon
1 tablespoon vegetable oil
½ cup *bulgur* (available at natural foods
   stores and most supermarkets)
¾ cup water
½ teaspoon salt
3 tablespoons chopped lightly toasted
   cashews

In a small heavy saucepan cook the onion with the coriander seed and the cinnamon in the oil over moderately low heat, stirring, until it is softened, add the *bulgur*, and cook the mixture, stirring, for 1 minute. Add the water and the salt, bring the liquid to a boil, and cook the mixture, covered, over low heat for 10 to 15 minutes, or until the liquid is absorbed. Stir in the cashews, remove the pan from the heat, and let the pilaf stand, covered, for 5 minutes. Serves 2.

Barley Pilaf with Mushrooms

1 cup chopped onion
¼ pound white mushrooms, sliced thin
½ bay leaf
2 tablespoons olive oil
½ cup pearl barley
1 cup water
1½ tablespoons minced fresh parsley leaves

In a small heavy saucepan cook the onion, the mushrooms, and the bay leaf in the oil over moderate heat, stirring, until the onion is soft and most of the liquid the mushrooms give off is evaporated. Stir in the barley, the water, and salt and pepper to taste, bring the water to a boil, and simmer the mixture, covered, for 30 to 35 minutes, or until the liquid is absorbed

and the barley is tender. Discard the bay leaf and with a fork stir in the parsley. Serves 2 generously.

Bulgur Pilaf with Scallion and Herbs

1 small onion, chopped
2 tablespoons unsalted butter
½ cup plus 2 tablespoons beef broth
½ cup water
¾ cup *bulgur* (available at natural foods
   stores and most supermarkets)
½ cup minced scallion
2 teaspoons minced fresh parsley leaves
2 teaspoons minced fresh basil leaves
2 teaspoons minced fresh mint leaves

In a heavy saucepan cook the onion in the butter over moderate heat, stirring, until it is softened. Add the broth, the water, and the *bulgur*, bring the liquid to a boil, and cook the mixture, covered, over low heat for 12 minutes, or until the liquid is absorbed. Remove the pan from the heat, let it stand, covered, for 5 minutes, and stir in the scallion, the parsley, the basil, the mint, and salt and pepper to taste. Serves 2 generously.

Couscous with Tomato and Chives

¾ cup chicken broth
1 tablespoon unsalted butter
½ cup couscous
1 plum tomato, seeded and chopped
1 tablespoon minced fresh chives

In a small saucepan bring the broth to a boil with the butter, stir in the couscous, and remove the pan from the heat. Let the couscous stand, covered, for 5 minutes, add the tomato, the chives, and salt and pepper to taste, and fluff the mixture with a fork. Serves 2.

Couscous Timbales with Pine Nuts, Jalapeño, and Chili Powder

1 tablespoon unsalted butter
¾ cup chicken broth
½ cup couscous
1 teaspoon minced seeded fresh or drained pickled *jalapeño* chili (wear rubber gloves)
1 tablespoon pine nuts, toasted lightly and chopped fine
1 tablespoon minced fresh parsley leaves
1½ tablespoons fresh lemon juice
½ teaspoon chili powder
3 tablespoons olive oil

In a saucepan combine the butter and the broth, bring the liquid to a boil, and stir in the couscous. Remove the pan from the heat, let the mixture stand, covered, for 5 minutes, and transfer it to a bowl. Break up any lumps with a fork and stir in the *jalapeño*, the pine nuts, the parsley, and salt and pepper to taste. In a small bowl whisk together the lemon juice, the chili powder, and the oil. Toss the couscous mixture with the dressing and season it with salt and pepper. Pack the couscous mixture into two ¾-cup timbales and unmold the timbales onto 2 plates. Serves 2.

Curried Couscous and Bell Pepper Timbales

½ onion, chopped fine
1 tablespoon unsalted butter
¾ teaspoon curry powder
3 tablespoons finely chopped green bell pepper
3 tablespoons finely chopped red bell pepper or drained bottled pimiento
⅓ cup chicken broth
⅓ cup couscous

In a skillet or small saucepan cook the onion in the butter over moderately low heat, stirring, until it is softened, add the curry powder, and cook the mixture, stirring, for 30 seconds. Add the bell peppers and cook the mixture, stirring, for 1 minute. Add the broth, bring the liquid to a boil, and stir in the couscous. Let the mixture stand, covered, off the heat for 5 minutes, season it with salt and pepper, and fluff it with a fork. Pack the couscous mixture into 2 well-buttered ⅔-cup timbale molds and invert the timbales onto a heated platter. Serves 2.

Photo on page 100

Kasha with Red Bell Pepper and Peanuts

½ cup chicken broth
½ cup water
1½ tablespoons olive oil
½ cup whole kasha
½ of a beaten large egg
1 small onion, chopped
1 small garlic clove, minced
1 small red bell pepper, chopped
2 tablespoons dry-roasted peanuts, finely
 chopped
2 tablespoons finely chopped scallion
plain yogurt for garnish

In a small saucepan combine the broth, the water, and ½ tablespoon of the oil and bring the liquid to a boil. In a bowl combine the kasha and the egg, stirring to coat the kasha well with the egg, transfer the mixture to a deep skillet with a lid, and cook the kasha over moderately high heat, stirring and breaking up the lumps, for 2 to 4 minutes, or until the grains are separated. Remove the skillet from the heat, add the broth mixture slowly (the mixture will spatter), and cover the skillet tightly. Cook the kasha, covered, over low heat for 10 to 15 minutes, or until the liquid is absorbed.

While the kasha is cooking, in a skillet cook the onion, the garlic, the red bell pepper, and salt and pepper to taste in the remaining 1 tablespoon oil over moderately low heat, stirring, until the vegetables are softened. Stir the vegetables into the kasha with the peanuts and the scallion and serve the kasha with a dollop of the yogurt. Serves 2.

Baked Polenta with Onions and Bacon

1 cup chicken broth
1 cup water
¼ teaspoon dried sage, crumbled
½ cup cornmeal
1 tablespoon unsalted butter, cut into bits
¼ cup freshly grated Parmesan
3 slices of bacon, chopped
2 onions, sliced thin

In a small heavy saucepan bring the broth and the water to a bare simmer with the sage, add the cornmeal in a stream, whisking constantly, and simmer the mixture, whisking vigorously, for 5 minutes. Whisk in the butter, 2 tablespoons of the Parmesan, and salt and pepper to taste, divide the polenta mixture between two buttered 1½-cup gratin dishes or spread it in a buttered 3-cup gratin dish, and bake it in the middle of a preheated 400° F. oven for 25 minutes.

While the polenta is baking, in a heavy skillet cook the bacon over moderate heat, stirring, until it is crisp, transfer it to paper towels to drain, and pour off all but 1 tablespoon of the fat. Cook the onions in the skillet over moderately low heat, stirring occasionally, until they are softened but not browned, and stir in the bacon.

Top the polenta with the onion mixture, spreading the onion mixture evenly, sprinkle it with the remaining 2 tablespoons Parmesan, and bake it in the oven for 5 minutes, or until the Parmesan is melted. Serves 2 as an entrée.

Photo on page 141

Fried Rice with Peas and Coriander

½ cup long-grain rice
¼ teaspoon salt
¾ cup water
½ tablespoons vegetable oil
1½ teaspoons grated peeled fresh gingerroot
½ cup thawed frozen peas
½ teaspoon Worcestershire sauce
2 teaspoons white-wine vinegar or distilled
  white vinegar
½ teaspoon sugar
¼ cup finely chopped fresh coriander

In a bowl wash the rice well in several changes of cold water and drain it in a sieve. In a small saucepan combine the rice, the salt, and the water and simmer the mixture, covered, for 18 minutes, or until the water is absorbed. Transfer the rice to a large shallow baking dish and chill it in the freezing compartment of the refrigerator for 10 minutes.

In a wok or heavy skillet heat the oil over high heat until it is hot but not smoking and in it stir-fry the gingerroot for 10 seconds, or until it is fragrant. Add the rice and the peas and stir-fry the mixture for 1 minute. Add the Worcestershire sauce, the vinegar, and the sugar and stir-fry the mixture for 1 minute, or until it is hot. Stir in the coriander and salt and pepper to taste. Serves 2.

Baked Polenta with Onions and Bacon

Mexican Rice Pilaf

⅔ cup chicken broth
½ cup water
1 plum tomato, seeded and quartered
1 small onion, chopped
1 garlic clove, minced
1 tablespoon vegetable oil
⅔ cup converted long-grain rice
½ teaspoon chili powder
½ teaspoon salt
1 tablespoon minced fresh coriander

In a blender blend the broth, the water, and the tomato until the mixture is smooth. In a heavy saucepan cook the onion and the garlic in the oil over moderately low heat, stirring, until the onion is softened, add the rice and the chili powder, and cook the mixture, stirring, for 1 minute. Stir in the tomato mixture and the salt, bring the liquid to a boil, and cook the mixture, covered, over low heat for 18 to 20 minutes, or until the liquid is absorbed. Fluff the pilaf with a fork, add the coriander, and let the pilaf stand, covered, off the heat for 5 minutes. Serves 2.

Crisp Shallot Rice

2 quarts water
½ teaspoon salt
⅔ cup long-grain rice (not converted)
vegetable oil for frying the shallots
¼ pound shallots, sliced thin
1 tablespoon unsalted butter

In a large saucepan bring the water to a boil with the salt. Sprinkle in the rice, stirring until the water returns to a boil, and boil it for 10 minutes. Drain the rice in a large colander and rinse it. Set the colander over a large saucepan of boiling water and steam the rice, covered with a kitchen towel and the lid, for 15 minutes, or until it is fluffy and dry. In a small skillet heat ½ inch of the oil over moderately

high heat until it is hot but not smoking, in it fry the shallots for 5 to 7 minutes, or until they are just golden, and transfer them with a slotted spoon to paper towels to drain. In a bowl toss the rice with the butter, the shallots, and salt and pepper to taste. Serves 2.

Spicy Rice Pilaf

1 small garlic clove, minced
1 tablespoon minced peeled fresh gingerroot
⅛ teaspoon dried hot red pepper flakes, or
to taste
2 teaspoons vegetable oil
⅔ cup converted rice
a 3-inch cinnamon stick
½ bay leaf
1⅓ cups water
¼ teaspoon salt
1 tablespoon minced fresh parsley leaves or
fresh coriander

In a small heavy saucepan cook the garlic, the gingerroot, and the red pepper flakes in the oil over moderately low heat for 1 minute, add the rice, the cinnamon stick, and the bay leaf, and cook the mixture over moderate heat, stirring, for 1 minute. Stir in the water and the salt, bring the liquid to a boil, and cook the rice, covered, over low heat for 18 to 20 minutes, or until the liquid is absorbed. Fluff the rice with a fork and let it stand, covered, off the heat for 5 minutes. Discard the cinnamon stick and the bay leaf and stir in the parsley. Serves 2.

Tipsy Rice

¾ cup beef broth
½ cup Tawny Port
½ teaspoon salt
½ cup long-grain rice
1 teaspoon dried orégano, crumbled
1 tablespoon unsalted butter, softened

In a saucepan combine the broth, the Port, and the salt, bring the liquid to a boil, and stir in the rice. Simmer the rice, covered, for 20 minutes, or until it is tender and the liquid is absorbed, and toss it with the orégano and the butter. Makes about 1½ cups, serving 2.

Corn and Bell Pepper Risotto with Basil

1½ cups chicken broth
½ cup water
¼ cup finely chopped onion
2 tablespoons unsalted butter
¾ cup long-grain rice
½ cup dry white wine or dry vermouth
1 small red bell pepper, chopped
1 cup corn kernels, thawed if frozen
1 tablespoon thinly sliced fresh basil leaves or
    1 teaspoon dried, crumbled
⅓ cup freshly grated Parmesan

In a saucepan bring the broth and the water to a simmer and keep it at a bare simmer. In a heavy saucepan cook the onion in the butter over moderately low heat, stirring, until it is softened. Add the rice, stirring with a wooden spatula until it is coated well with the butter, add the wine, and cook the mixture over moderately high heat, stirring, until the wine is absorbed. Add about ½ cup of the simmering broth and cook the mixture, stirring, until the broth is absorbed. Continue adding the broth, about ½ cup at a time, stirring constantly and letting each portion be absorbed before adding the next. With the last ½ cup broth add the bell pepper, the corn, and the basil, stirring, and cook the mixture until the broth is absorbed and the rice is *al dente*. (The rice should take a total of about 18 minutes to become *al dente*.) Remove the pan from the heat and stir in the Parmesan and salt and pepper to taste. Serves 2.

Lemon Broccoli Risotto

4 cups chicken broth
2 cups water
1 pound broccoli, cut into flowerets, quartered if large, and stems cut into ½-inch dice
1 teaspoon freshly grated lemon zest
1 tablespoon fresh lemon juice
1 small onion, chopped fine
1 small garlic clove, minced
2 tablespoons olive oil
1½ cups rice (short-, medium-, or long-grain)
½ cup freshly grated Parmesan

In a large saucepan bring the broth and the water to a boil and in the broth simmer the broccoli flowerets for 3 minutes, or until they are just tender. Transfer the flowerets with a skimmer to a bowl and reserve them. To the simmering broth add the broccoli stems, the zest, and the lemon juice and simmer the mixture for 5 minutes. While the stems are cooking, in a large heavy saucepan cook the onion and the garlic in the oil over moderately low heat, stirring, until the onion is softened and stir in the rice, stirring until each grain is coated with the oil. Add ½ cup of the simmering broth, stems included, and cook the mixture over moderately high heat, stirring constantly, until the broth is absorbed. Continue adding the broth mixture, ½ cup at a time, stirring constantly and letting each portion be absorbed before adding the next, until the rice is tender but still *al dente*. (The rice should take abut 20 minutes to become *al dente*.) Stir in the reserved broccoli flowerets and simmer the risotto, stirring, until the flowerets are heated through. Remove the pan from the heat and stir in the Parmesan and salt and pepper to taste. Serves 2 as an entrée.

Photo on page 136

Cauliflower and Spinach Vinaigrette

VEGETABLES

Bright red ripe tomatoes, sweet yellow corn, crispy orange carrots… fresh vegetables are filled with flavor, bursting with color, and loaded with vitamins and nutrients. They are among the most delicious *and* healthful foods you can eat.

Vegetables should always be bought fresh, and, more important, in season.
Try to buy produce at its peak, even if it is available year-round. For example, do not feel compelled to purchase asparagus in October, wait until the spring months when it will be at its tender best. Here's a quick guide to help you use some of nature's bounty in its prime:

> *Spring:* artichokes, asparagus, broccoli, escarole, endive
> *Summer:* green beans, corn, eggplant, tomatoes, zucchini
> *Fall:* broccoli (again), Brussels sprouts, cauliflower, squash
> *Winter:* cabbage, kale, turnips, winter squash

Good quality carrots, bell peppers, potatoes, and spinach are available throughout the year. When selecting your produce, look for firm, tight vegetables free of bruises or soft spots and with dark, full color. Also, never be tempted to buy precut fresh vegetables; they are often dried out and stale.

You'll notice that a few of our recipes call for a steamer to prepare vegetables. Steaming wonderfully retains the vibrant taste, crisp-tender texture, and bright colors of fresh vegetables. We recommend a collapsible steamer rack, an inexpensive kind of wire basket that adjusts to fit any pot. If you do not have a steamer, use a colander set over simmering water instead.

145

Artichokes with Anchovy, Egg, and Parsley Sauce

2 medium artichokes
½ lemon
¼ cup packed flat-leafed parsley leaves
1 small garlic clove, chopped
2 flat anchovy fillets, drained
2 tablespoons fresh lemon juice
¼ cup plus 2 tablespoons olive oil
1 hard-boiled egg, chopped

Break off and discard the stems and tough outer leaves of the artichokes and trim the bases. Cut off the top quarter of each artichoke with a very sharp stainless-steel knife, snip off the sharp tips of the leaves with scissors, and rub the cut surfaces with the lemon half. In a saucepan simmer the artichokes in 1½ inches boiling salted water, covered, for 25 to 30 minutes, or until the stem ends are tender. Drain the artichokes, inverted, on paper towels.

While the artichokes are cooling, in a blender or food processor blend the parsley, the garlic, the anchovies, the lemon juice, and salt to taste until the mixture forms a paste. With the motor running add the oil in a stream and blend the sauce until it is emulsified. Stir the hard-boiled egg into the sauce and divide the sauce between 2 small bowls. Serve the artichokes warm or at room temperature with the sauce. Serves 2 as a side dish or a first course.

Asparagus with Cream Sauce

¾ pound asparagus, trimmed and the bottom
   2 inches of each stalk peeled
3 large egg yolks
3 tablespoons unsalted butter, melted
1 cup well-chilled heavy cream
freshly ground white pepper to taste
3 tablespoons cream cheese, softened
2½ tablespoons fresh lemon juice

In a kettle of boiling salted water cook the asparagus for 4 to 6 minutes, or until the stalks are tender but not limp, in a colander refresh it under cold water, and let it drain.

In a metal bowl set over barely simmering water combine the egg yolks, the butter, ½ cup of the cream, the white pepper, and salt to taste and cook the mixture, whisking, until it is pale and thick. (Do not let the mixture boil.) Remove the metal bowl from the pan of simmering water, whisk in the cream cheese and the lemon juice, and let the mixture cool.

In a chilled bowl beat the remaining ½ cup cream until it holds stiff peaks and fold it into the egg mixture. Arrange the asparagus on a platter and spoon ½ cup of the sauce over it. *(The leftover sauce keeps, covered and chilled, for up to 2 days and can be served with cooled steamed vegetables.)* Serves 2 as a side dish or a first course.

Black Bean and Cheddar Burritos with Spicy Tomato Sauce

a 14- to 16-ounce can whole tomatoes,
    drained
1 garlic clove, chopped
1 tablespoon minced seeded fresh or
    pickled *jalapeño* chili (wear rubber gloves),
    or to taste
four 10-inch flour tortillas
1 cup drained canned black beans
¼ cup finely chopped red onion
¼ cup finely chopped green bell pepper
1 cup grated sharp Cheddar (about ¼ pound)
2 tablespoons chopped fresh coriander plus
    sprigs for garnish, if desired

In a blender purée the tomatoes with the garlic and the *jalapeño* and transfer the sauce to a small saucepan. Simmer the sauce for 10 to 15 minutes, or until it is thickened, and keep it warm.

Working with 1 tortilla at a time, spread ¼ cup of the beans in a line down the center of each tortilla, top the beans with 1 tablespoon of the red onion, 1 tablespoon of the bell pepper, and ¼ cup of the Cheddar, and roll the tortilla gently around the filling to enclose the filling. Transfer the *burritos* carefully, seam sides down, to a baking dish large enough to hold them in one layer. Cover the baking dish tightly with foil and bake the *burritos* in a preheated 400° F. oven for 10 to 15 minutes, or until they are heated through.

Stir the coriander into the sauce. Transfer the *burritos* with a spatula to 2 heated plates, spoon some of the sauce over them, and garnish the servings with the coriander sprigs. Serve the *burritos* with the remaining sauce. Serves 2 as an entrée.

Green Beans with Mushroom Butter

2 tablespoons unsalted butter, softened
⅓ cup minced mushrooms
1 teaspoon minced fresh parsley leaves
1 small garlic clove, minced
½ pound green beans, trimmed

In a small bowl combine well the butter, the mushrooms, the parsley, the garlic, and salt and pepper to taste. In a steamer set over boiling water steam the beans, covered partially, for 8 to 15 minutes, or until they are crisp-tender, transfer them to a heated serving dish, and toss them with the mushroom butter. Serves 2.

Lima Bean Purée with Olive Oil and Orégano

a 10-ounce package frozen lima beans
¼ cup water
2 teaspoons extra-virgin olive oil
½ teaspoon white-wine vinegar
¼ teaspoon dried orégano, crumbled
a pinch of sugar
toasted garlic bread as an accompaniment
    if desired

In a saucepan combine the lima beans and the water, bring the water to a boil, breaking up the beans, and simmer the beans, covered, for 8 minutes. Transfer the beans with the liquid to a food processor, add the oil, the vinegar, the orégano, the sugar, and salt and pepper to taste, and purée the mixture until it is smooth. Serve the purée as a spread on the garlic toast or as a side dish. Serves 2.

147

Sliced Beets with Citrus Butter

¾ **pound beets without the stems,
   peeled and sliced ¼ inch thick**
2 **tablespoons unsalted butter, cut into pieces**
3 **tablespoons fresh orange juice**
1 **tablespoon fresh lemon juice**
2 **teaspoons sugar**
1 **teaspoon orange zest**
1 **tablespoon finely chopped fresh parsley
   leaves**

In a large skillet combine the beets with the butter, 1 cup water, and salt to taste, bring the liquid to a boil, and simmer the beets, covered, for 12 minutes. Simmer the beets, uncovered, adding more water if necessary, for 8 to 10 minutes more, or until they are tender and almost all the liquid is evaporated. Add the orange juice, the lemon juice, the sugar, the orange zest, and salt and pepper to taste. Simmer the mixture until the liquid is reduced to a glaze and stir in the parsley. Serves 2.

Steamed Broccoli with Spicy Peanuts and Lime

½ **pound broccoli, separated into flowerets
   and the stems sliced thin crosswise**
1 **small garlic clove, minced**
¼ **teaspoon dried hot red pepper flakes**
2 **tablespoons unsalted butter**
1½ **tablespoons finely chopped peanuts**
1 **teaspoon fresh lime juice, or to taste**

In a steamer set over simmering water steam the broccoli, covered, for 4 to 6 minutes, or until it is crisp-tender. In a small heavy skillet cook the garlic with the red pepper flakes in the butter, stirring, over moderate heat, until it is golden, add the peanuts, the lime juice, and salt to taste, and cook the mixture, stirring, for 1 minute. Transfer the broccoli to a bowl, add the peanut mixture, and toss the broccoli to coat it. Serves 2.

Broccoli with Sunflower Seeds

2 **tablespoons shelled unsalted sunflower
   seeds**
2 **tablespoons olive oil**
¼ **cup minced onion**
4 **cups (about ½ bunch) broccoli flowerets**
1 **tablespoon soy sauce**
2 **tablespoons water**

In a heavy skillet sauté the sunflower seeds in the oil over moderately high heat, stirring, until they are golden and drain them on paper towels. In the oil remaining in the skillet sauté the onion over moderately high heat until it is browned, add the broccoli, and toss it to coat it with the oil. Add the soy sauce and the water and cook the broccoli, covered, over moderately low heat for 3 minutes, or until the broccoli is tender and the liquid is evaporated. Transfer the broccoli to a heated serving dish and sprinkle it with the sunflower seeds. Serves 2.

Cajun-Style Cabbage

3 **slices of bacon**
5 **cups coarsely chopped cabbage
   (about 1 small head)**
½ **cup water**
cayenne to taste

In a large heavy skillet cook the bacon over moderate heat, turning it once, until it is crisp, transfer it to paper towels to drain, and crumble it. Pour off all but 2 tablespoons of the fat from the skillet and heat the remaining fat over moderately high heat until it is hot. Add the cabbage and sauté it, stirring, for 5 to 8 minutes, or until it is browned. Add the water, cook the mixture, covered, for 8 to 10 minutes, or until the cabbage is tender, and stir in the cayenne, the bacon, and salt to taste. Transfer the cabbage mixture to a heated serving dish. Serves 2.

Honey-Glazed Baby Carrots

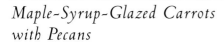

½ pound baby carrots, trimmed and peeled
1 tablespoon unsalted butter
1 tablespoon honey

In a steamer set over boiling water steam the carrots, covered, for 4 to 8 minutes, or until they are just tender. In a small skillet melt the butter with the honey over moderately low heat, add the carrots and salt and pepper to taste, and cook the carrots, tossing them, for 1 minute, or until they are well-coated with the glaze. Serves 2.

Photo on front jacket

Maple-Syrup-Glazed Carrots with Pecans

½ pound carrots, cut on the diagonal into ¼-inch slices
1 tablespoon unsalted butter
2 tablespoons maple syrup
¾ cup water
1 teaspoon fresh lemon juice, or to taste
¼ teaspoon salt
2 teaspoons minced lightly toasted pecans

In a skillet combine the carrots, the butter, the syrup, and the water and boil the mixture, shaking the skillet occasionally, until almost all the liquid is evaporated. Add the lemon juice and the salt, cook the mixture over low heat, stirring, for 30 seconds, or until the carrots are coated well with the glaze, and sprinkle the carrots with the pecans. Serves 2.

Cauliflower Purée with Roquefort

1 small head of cauliflower, separated into flowerets (about 4 cups) and the tough stems discarded
¼ cup milk
2 shallots, minced (about 2 tablespoons)
freshly ground white pepper to taste
¼ cup crumbled Roquefort
1½ teaspoons white-wine vinegar, or to taste
2 teaspoons minced fresh chives

In a large saucepan cook the cauliflower in boiling salted water to cover for 10 minutes, or until it is very tender. In a small saucepan stir together the milk, the shallots, the white pepper, and salt to taste and simmer the mixture for 5 minutes. In a food processor purée the cauliflower with the milk mixture, the Roquefort, and the vinegar until the mixture is smooth. Transfer the purée to a serving bowl and top it with the chives. Serve the purée with grilled steaks or veal chops. Serves 2.

Cauliflower and Spinach Vinaigrette

2 tablespoons red-wine vinegar
2 tablespoons finely chopped pimiento-
  stuffed green olives
2 tablespoons finely chopped bottled roasted
  red peppers
1 tablespoon finely chopped fresh parsley
  leaves (preferably flat-leafed)
3 tablespoons olive oil
1 small head of cauliflower, separated into
  flowerets (about 4 cups)
6 ounces spinach, washed well and coarse
  stems discarded

In a small bowl whisk together the vinegar, the olives, the roasted peppers, the parsley, and salt to taste, add the oil, whisking, and whisk the dressing until it is emulsified.

In a saucepan of boiling salted water cook the cauliflower for 8 to 10 minutes, or until it is tender, and drain it well. To the saucepan add the spinach with the water clinging to its leaves and cook it, covered, over moderately high heat for 3 minutes, or until it is wilted. Blot the spinach dry with a triple layer of paper towels, pressing out the excess liquid. Transfer the spinach to a platter, mound the cauliflower on it, and spoon the dressing over the vegetables. Serve the vegetables at room temperature. Serves 2.

Photo on page 144

Cajun-Style Corn

3 ears of corn
½ cup sliced onion
2 tablespoons unsalted butter
4 to 5 tablespoons heavy cream
cayenne to taste

Cut the corn kernels from the cobs with a serrated knife and scrape the remaining corn from the cobs with the back of the knife. In a saucepan cook the onion in the butter over moderately high heat, stirring occasionally, until it is browned lightly, add the corn and 4 tablespoons of the cream, and cook the mixture, covered, over low heat, stirring occasionally, for 20 minutes. (If the mixture begins to stick, add the remaining 1 tablespoon cream.) Season the corn mixture with the cayenne and salt and black pepper to taste. Serves 2.

Brown Buttered Corn with Basil

1 tablespoon unsalted butter
1½ cups fresh corn (cut from about 3 ears)
½ cup finely shredded fresh basil leaves

In a skillet heat the butter over moderately high heat until the foam subsides, and in it sauté the corn, stirring, for 4 minutes, or until it is browned partially. Remove the skillet from the heat and stir in the basil and salt and pepper to taste. Serves 2.

Photo on page 26

Creamed Corn and Red Bell Pepper

1½ cups fresh corn kernels (cut from
  about 2 large ears)
1 tablespoon olive oil
½ cup finely chopped red bell pepper
3 tablespoons heavy cream or half-and-half

In a heavy skillet cook the corn in the oil over moderately high heat, stirring, for 3 minutes. Add the bell pepper, and cook the mixture, stirring, for 3 to 4 minutes more, or until the vegetables are tender. Add the cream and salt and pepper to taste and simmer the mixture until the cream is almost evaporated. Serves 2.

Photo on page 68

Sautéed Endive and Romaine

1½ teaspoons minced garlic
3 tablespoons olive oil
1 pound romaine, rinsed, dried, and chopped
1 Belgian endive, trimmed and chopped

In a large saucepan cook the garlic in the oil over moderately low heat for 30 seconds, add the romaine and the endive, and stir the mixture well to coat it with the oil. Cook the vegetables over moderate heat, stirring, for 6 to 7 minutes, or until they are wilted and tender, and season them with salt and pepper to taste. Serves 2.

Sautéed Kale with Olives

¾ pound kale, stems discarded and the leaves chopped coarse
1 tablespoon vegetable oil or olive oil
6 Kalamata olives, pitted and sliced
1 teaspoon fresh lemon juice, or to taste

In a large bowl of ice and generously salted cold water let the kale soak for 15 minutes, drain it, and spin it dry. In a large skillet heat the oil over moderately high heat until it is hot but not smoking, add the kale with salt and pepper to taste, and sauté it, stirring, for 3 to 5 minutes, or until it is wilted. Stir in the olives and the lemon juice and sauté the mixture for 15 seconds. Serves 2.

Red Pepper and Eggplant Vinaigrette

For the dressing
1 garlic clove minced and mashed to a paste with ¼ teaspoon salt
2 tablespoons wine vinegar
¼ teaspoon pepper
⅓ cup olive oil
¼ teaspoon Dijon-style mustard

1 small eggplant (about ½ pound), cut lengthwise into ½-inch slices
1 red bell pepper, quartered lengthwise and the stem, seeds, and ribs discarded
olive oil for brushing the vegetables

Make the dressing: In a bowl combine the garlic paste with the vinegar and the pepper. Add the oil in a stream, whisking, and whisk the dressing until it is emulsified. Whisk in the mustard.

Brush the eggplant and the red pepper slices with the oil and broil them in a jelly-roll pan under a preheated broiler about 4 inches from the heat for 3 to 4 minutes on each side, or until the eggplant is browned and the pepper skin is charred. Slice the eggplant lengthwise in ½-inch-wide strips. Peel the peppers and slice them lengthwise into ¼-inch-wide strips. Whisk the dressing and toss the eggplant and the pepper with it. Serves 2.

151

Crusty Caraway Potato Galette with Cheese

1 tablespoon unsalted butter, melted
1 tablespoon vegetable oil
¾ pound boiling or baking potatoes, scrubbed but not peeled
½ teaspoon caraway seeds
½ cup grated Gruyère

In a small bowl stir together the butter and the vegetable oil. In a food processor fitted with a 1-millimeter slicing blade or with a *mandoline* or similar hand-held slicing device, slice the potatoes thin. Working quickly to prevent the potatoes from discoloring, brush the bottom of an 8½- to 9-inch heavy ovenproof skillet, preferably non-stick, with some of the butter mixture and cover it with a layer of the potato slices, overlapping them. Brush the potatoes with some of the remaining butter mixture, sprinkle them with some of the caraway seeds, and season them with salt and pepper. Layer the remaining potatoes with the remaining butter mixture and the remaining caraway seeds, and season them with salt and pepper in the same manner. Heat the mixture over moderately high heat until it begins to sizzle, transfer the skillet to the middle of a preheated 450° F. oven, and bake the *galette* for 25 minutes, or until it is golden and the potatoes are tender. Sprinkle the Gruyère over the galette and bake it for 3 minutes, or until it is bubbling and golden. Cut the *galette* into wedges. Serves 2.

Garlic Mashed Potatoes

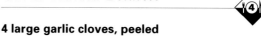

4 large garlic cloves, peeled
1 pound russet (baking) potatoes, peeled and cut into 1-inch pieces
3 tablespoons unsalted butter, or to taste, cut into bits and softened

In a steamer set over boiling water steam the garlic with the potatoes, covered, for 15 minutes, or until the potatoes are tender, remove the steamer from the pan, and pour off the steaming liquid, reserving it. Force the steamed potatoes and garlic through a ricer or food mill into the pan and stir in the butter and ⅓ to ½ cup of the reserved steaming liquid, or enough to achieve the desired consistency. Season the potatoes with salt and pepper to taste and heat them over low heat, stirring, until they are hot. Serves 2.

Herbed New Potatoes

¾ pound small boiling potatoes, quartered
1 tablespoon minced fresh parsley leaves
1 tablespoon minced fresh mint leaves
1 tablespoon snipped fresh chives
2 tablespoons unsalted butter, softened

In a steamer set over boiling water steam the potatoes, covered, for 10 minutes, or until they are just tender. In a bowl toss the potatoes gently with the parsley, the mint, the chives, the butter, and the salt and pepper to taste. Serves 2.

Photo on front jacket

Spinach, Bacon, and Mushroom Gratin

2 slices of bacon, cut into ½-inch pieces
¼ pound white mushrooms, sliced thin
a 10-ounce package fresh spinach, washed
    well and coarse stems discarded
¼ cup freshly grated Parmesan
1 large egg, beaten lightly
1½ teaspoons fresh lemon juice
14 saltine crackers, ground fine in a food
    processor or blender
1 tablespoon unsalted butter, melted

In a large skillet cook the bacon over moderate heat, stirring, until it is crisp and pour off all but 1 tablespoon of the fat. Add the mushrooms and sauté them, stirring, over moderately high heat until the liquid they give off is evaporated. Transfer the bacon and mushrooms to a bowl. Add the spinach to the pan and cook it in the water clinging to the leaves, covered, over moderately high heat for 3 minutes, or until it is wilted, and drain it well. Add the spinach to the bowl with 3 tablespoons of the Parmesan, the egg, the lemon juice, 2 tablespoons of the ground crackers, and salt and pepper to taste and spoon the spinach mixture into a buttered shallow 2-cup baking dish. In a small bowl combine well the remaining ground crackers with the butter and the remaining 1 tablespoon Parmesan, sprinkle the cracker topping over the spinach mixture, and bake the gratin in the middle of a preheated 425° F. oven for 15 minutes, or until the top is golden. Serves 2 as a luncheon entrée or side dish.

Acorn Squash in Honey Bourbon Sauce

1 acorn squash, halved lengthwise, seeded,
    peeled, and cut into 1-inch-thick slices
½ stick (¼ cup) unsalted butter, cut into pieces
2 tablespoons bourbon
3 tablespoons honey
1 teaspoon grated orange zest
3 tablespoons water

In a gratin dish arrange the squash in one layer. In a saucepan combine the butter, the bourbon, the honey, the orange zest, and the water, bring the mixture to a boil over high heat, stirring, and ladle the sauce over the squash. Bake the squash, covered with foil, in a preheated 400° F. oven for 20 to 25 minutes, or until it is tender and the sauce is thickened. Divide the squash between serving dishes and spoon the sauce over it. Serves 2.

153

Zucchini with Yogurt, Scallion, and Dill

½ pound zucchini, scrubbed, trimmed,
    halved lengthwise, and cut into
    ¼-inch slices
1 tablespoon unsalted butter
¼ cup plain yogurt stirred with ½ teaspoon
    cornstarch
2 tablespoons finely chopped scallion
1 tablespoon finely chopped fresh dill

In a skillet cook the zucchini in the butter, covered, over moderately low heat, stirring occasionally, for 5 to 7 minutes, or until it is crisp-tender, add the yogurt mixture, the scallion, the dill, and salt and pepper to taste, and cook the mixture, stirring, for 30 seconds, or just until the zucchini is coated well. (The sauce may appear slightly curdled.) Serves 2.

Turnip Scallion Soufflés

1 tablespoon thinly sliced white part of
    scallion and 2 tablespoons thinly sliced
    green part of scallion
1½ teaspoons olive oil
6 ounces turnips, peeled and chopped fine
    (about 2 cups)
3 tablespoons whole-milk ricotta
1 tablespoon freshly grated Gruyère
2 large eggs, separated
cayenne to taste
a pinch of cream of tartar
fine dry bread crumbs for dusting the dishes

In a heavy skillet cook the white part of the scallion in the oil over moderately low heat, stirring, until it is softened, add the turnips and ½ cup water, and cook the mixture, covered, over moderately high heat, adding more water if necessary, for 3 to 5 minutes, or until the water is evaporated and the turnips are tender. In a food processor purée the mixture with the ricotta and the Gruyère and transfer the mixture to a large bowl. Whisk in the egg yolks and the scallion greens and season the mixture with the cayenne and salt to taste. In a bowl beat the egg whites with the cream of tartar and a pinch of salt with a whisk until they form soft peaks, stir one fourth of the egg whites into the turnip mixture, and fold in the remaining egg whites gently but thoroughly. Dust 2 well-buttered and chilled 1-cup soufflé dishes with the bread crumbs and fill them with the turnip mixture. Bake the soufflés on a baking sheet in a preheated 425° F. oven for 15 to 20 minutes, or until they are puffed and golden. Serves 2.

Vegetable Pita Pizzas

two 6-inch whole-wheat *pita* loaves
3 tablespoons olive oil plus additional
    for brushing the *pita* rounds
1⅓ cups grated mozzarella
1 small red onion, sliced thin
2 garlic cloves, minced
1 small red bell pepper, sliced thin
1 small green bell pepper, sliced thin
¾ cup thinly sliced zucchini
4 mushrooms, sliced
1 teaspoon dried orégano, crumbled
⅔ cup chopped seeded fresh tomato
3 tablespoons shredded fresh basil leaves
3 tablespoons freshly grated Parmesan

Halve the *pita* loaves horizontally to form 4 rounds, arrange the rounds, rough sides up, on a baking sheet, and brush the tops lightly with the additional oil. Sprinkle the rounds with salt to taste and toast them in the middle of a preheated 350° F. oven for 5 minutes, or until they are pale golden and crisp. Sprinkle half the mozzarella onto the rounds and bake the rounds for 1 minute, or until the mozzarella is melted. While the rounds are toasting, in a large skillet cook the onion and the garlic in the remaining 3 tablespoons oil over moderately low heat, stirring, until the onion is softened, add the bell peppers, and cook the mixture, stirring, for 4 minutes, or until the peppers are softened. Add the zucchini, the mushrooms, the orégano, and salt and black pepper to taste and cook the mixture, stirring, for 2 minutes, or until the zucchini is softened. Stir in half the remaining mozzarella and divide the mixture among the rounds, mounding it slightly. Top the rounds with the remaining mozzarella, the tomato, the basil, and the Parmesan and broil the rounds under a preheated broiler about 4 inches from the heat for 3 minutes, or until the cheeses are melted and bubbly. Makes 4 pizzas, serving 2 as a light entrée.

Photo on page 155

Vegetable Pita Pizzas

Vegetable Ribbons with Horseradish Lemon Butter

1 carrot, peeled
1 small zucchini, scrubbed
1 small yellow summer squash, washed well
1 tablespoon unsalted butter
½ teaspoon drained bottled horseradish
1 teaspoon fresh lemon juice

With a vegetable peeler cut the carrot, the zucchini, and the yellow summer squash lengthwise into "ribbons," reserving the center cores for another use. In a heavy skillet cook the vegetables in the butter over moderately high heat, stirring, for 1 to 2 minutes, or until the vegetables are crisp-tender, add the horseradish, the lemon juice, and salt and pepper to taste, and toss the mixture well. Serves 2.

Photo on page 32

Sardine and Watercress Salad with Shredded Potato Cake

SALADS

ot so very long ago, salad meant wedges of iceberg lettuce, period.

Not so very long ago, salad meant wedges of iceberg lettuce, period. But today, salads are not strictly green or just side dishes. Entrée salads, for example, use greens along with fresh herbs, crisp vegetables, meats, poultry, and fish to create irresistible lunches or light dinners. Our Lobster Salad with Basil and Lemon Vinaigrette; Sardine and Watercress Salad with Shredded Potato Cake; and Spicy Asian Steak Salad are all as delectable as they are beautiful.

We also offer salads of vegetables, pastas, and grains. These include both entrées and side dishes and are filled with bright color and flavor. Our Tomato, Cucumber, and Feta Salad; Tortellini Salad with Arugula; and Rice and Pine Nut Salad are just a sampling.

When you are in the mood for a green salad, look for red leaf, green leaf, Boston, Bibb, and cos lettuces, or chicory, endive, escarole, radicchio, arugula, watercress, and more. Produce-market shelves are packed with these delicious multi-colored, -textured, and -flavored greens. We encourage you to mix-and-match them daily with your own favorite dressing for a healthful complement to any meal. Our simple recipes such as Escarole Salad with Honey Lime Dressing, and Watercress, Endive, and Goat Cheese Salad will get you started. The only piece of equipment we encourage you to buy is a salad-spinner to thoroughly dry your salad greens, keeping them crisp and allowing them to hold dressings well without getting soggy. And remember to dress and toss your greens just before serving to ensure crispness.

Entrée Salads
❧ ❧ ❧

Chicken, Apple, and Celery Salad

**1 whole skinless boneless chicken breast
   (1 pound), or 1½ cups cubed cooked chicken**
2 teaspoons honey
2 teaspoons cider vinegar
1 cup mayonnaise
1 rib of celery, chopped
1 cup chopped unpeeled red apple
½ cup diced Swiss cheese
½ teaspoon celery seeds
lettuce leaves for lining the plates

If using the uncooked chicken breast, in a saucepan cover the chicken with water, bring the water to a boil, and simmer the chicken, covered partially, for 12 minutes, or until it is firm to the touch and just cooked through. Transfer the chicken to a plate, let it cool, and cut it into ¾-inch cubes.

In a small bowl dissolve the honey in the vinegar and whisk the mixture into the mayonnaise. In a bowl toss the cubed cooked chicken, the celery, the apple, the cheese, and the celery seeds with the mayonnaise mixture and divide the salad between plates lined with the lettuce. Serves 2.

Chicken and Grape Salad with Cashews

2 tablespoons fresh lime juice
**1 tablespoon Major Grey's chutney,
   minced if necessary**
**1 small garlic clove, minced and mashed
   to a paste with ¼ teaspoon salt**
2 tablespoons sour cream
3 tablespoons vegetable oil
1 to 2 drops of Tabasco
1½ cups shredded cooked chicken
1 cup seedless green or red grapes, halved
½ cup roasted salted cashew nuts
**2 cups watercress sprigs, coarse stems
   discarded, rinsed well and spun dry**

In a small bowl whisk together the lime juice, the chutney, the garlic paste, and the sour cream, add the oil in a stream, whisking until the dressing is emulsified, and whisk in the Tabasco. In a bowl toss the chicken and the grapes with the dressing and let the mixture marinate for 15 minutes. In a salad bowl toss together gently the cashews, the watercress, the chicken mixture, and salt and pepper to taste and divide the salad between 2 plates. Serves 2.

Lentil Salad with Smoked Salmon and Arugula

¾ cup lentils, picked over
½ teaspoon dried thyme, crumbled
1 small onion, quartered
a pinch of ground allspice
2 tablespoons white-wine vinegar
1 teaspoon Dijon-style mustard
¼ cup olive oil
⅓ cup minced celery
⅓ cup minced carrot
½ cup minced fresh parsley leaves
**6 ounces thinly sliced smoked salmon,
   cut into 12 strips**
12 *arugula* leaves, rinsed and patted dry

In a large saucepan of boiling water boil the lentils with the thyme, the onion, and the allspice for 15 to 20 minutes, or until they are just tender, and drain the mixture in a sieve. Discard the onion, rinse the lentils under gently running water, and drain them well. In a bowl whisk together the vinegar, the mustard, and salt and pepper to taste, add the oil in a stream, whisking, and whisk the dressing until it is emulsified. Stir in the lentils, the celery, the carrot, and the parsley. Arrange the salmon and the *arugula* decoratively on 2 plates and divide the lentil salad between the plates. Serves 2.

Photo on this page

Lentil Salad with Smoked Salmon and Arugula

Lobster Salad with Basil and Lemon Vinaigrette

two 1¼- to 1½-pound live lobsters
½ pound peas, shelled (about ½ cup)
½ cup diagonally sliced celery
1 tablespoon minced fresh basil leaves
1 tablespoon freshly grated lemon zest
3 tablespoons fresh lemon juice
⅓ cup olive oil
white pepper to taste

For garnish
4 small lettuce leaves
4 lemon slices
4 tomato slices

Into a kettle of boiling salted water plunge the live lobsters and boil them, covered, for 8 minutes from the time the water returns to a boil. Transfer the lobsters with tongs to a cutting board and let them cool until they can be handled. Break off the claws at the body, crack them, and remove the meat, cutting it into ¾-inch pieces. Halve the lobsters lengthwise along the undersides, remove the meat from the tails, and cut it into ¾-inch pieces. In a large bowl combine the claw meat and the tail meat. Break off the legs carefully at the body, reserving them for another use, remove the meat from the body cavities near the leg joints, and add it to the bowl.

In a saucepan of boiling salted water cook the peas for 5 minutes, or until they are just tender, drain them in a colander, and refresh them under cold water. Pat the peas dry and add them to the lobster. Stir in the celery, the basil, and the lemon zest. In a small bowl whisk the lemon juice with a pinch of salt, add the oil in a stream, whisking, and whisk the dressing until it is emulsified. Drizzle the lobster mixture with the dressing, toss it to coat it well, and add salt and white pepper to taste. Divide the salad between 2 plates and garnish it with the lettuce and the lemon and tomato slices. Serves 2.

Photo on page 161

Shrimp, Snow Pea, and Red Pepper Salad in Fresh Ginger Dressing

½ pound snow peas, trimmed and strings discarded
½ red bell pepper, cut into julienne strips
½ pound small shrimp (about 24)
¼ cup plain yogurt
2 tablespoons mayonnaise
1 tablespoon minced peeled fresh gingerroot
1 teaspoon Dijon-style mustard
1 teaspoon fresh lemon juice, or to taste
½ teaspoon sugar
soft lettuce leaves for lining the plate

In a saucepan of boiling salted water blanch the snow peas and the bell pepper for 15 seconds and transfer them with a slotted spoon to a bowl of ice and cold water to stop the cooking. Drain the vegetables, pat them dry, and cut the snow peas lengthwise into julienne strips.

To the pan of boiling salted water add the shrimp, remove the pan from the heat, and let the shrimp stand, covered, for 5 minutes. Drain the shrimp in a colander and refresh them under cold water until they are cool. Shell the shrimp and, if desired, devein them. In a bowl whisk together the yogurt, the mayonnaise, the gingerroot, the mustard, the lemon juice, the sugar, and salt and pepper to taste and stir in the shrimp and the vegetables. Divide the salad between 2 plates lined with the lettuce leaves. Serves 2.

Sardine and Watercress Salad with Shredded Potato Cake

For the dressing
1 tablespoon white-wine vinegar, or to taste
1 tablespoon Dijon-style mustard, or to taste
¼ cup olive oil
1 tablespoon water

a ½-pound russet (baking) potato
1 tablespoon unsalted butter
1 small bunch of watercress, coarse stems
   discarded, rinsed well and spun dry
   (about 3 cups)
½ red onion, sliced thin, separated into rings,
   and soaked in ice water to cover for
   30 minutes
a 3¾-ounce can brisling sardines packed in
   oil, drained well

Make the dressing: In a small bowl whisk together the vinegar, the mustard, and salt and pepper to taste, add the oil in a stream, whisking, and whisk in the water.

Peel the potato, grate it coarse, and squeeze it between several thicknesses of paper towels to remove any excess moisture. In a non-stick skillet measuring 6 inches across the bottom heat ½ tablespoon of the butter over moderately high heat until the foam subsides, add half the potato, tamping it down with a spatula, and cook the potato cake, shaking the skillet frequently to keep the potato from sticking, for 6 minutes, or until the underside is golden and crisp. Turn the potato cake, cook it for 6 minutes more, or until the underside is golden and crisp, and transfer it to a plate. Make a second potato cake in the same manner with the remaining butter and potato and transfer it to another plate. In a bowl toss the watercress with 3 tablespoons of the dressing and spoon the remaining dressing around the potato cakes. Arrange the onion, drained well, the watercress, and the sardines decoratively on the potato cakes. Serves 2.

Photo on page 156

Lobster Salad with Basil and Lemon Vinaigrette

Spicy Asian Steak Salad

1 tablespoon Worcestershire sauce
3 tablespoons fresh lime juice
¼ teaspoon cayenne
1 tablespoon sugar
1 tablespoon soy sauce
1 garlic clove, minced and mashed to a paste
  with ½ teaspoon salt
¾ pound flank steak, cut diagonally against
  the grain into ¼-inch-thick strips
2 tablespoons vegetable oil
3 cups mung bean sprouts, rinsed and
  drained well
½ small red onion, halved lengthwise and
  sliced thin lengthwise
½ cup chopped fresh coriander or
  fresh mint leaves
soft lettuce leaves for lining the plates
lime wedges for garnish

In a bowl whisk together the Worcestershire sauce, the lime juice, the cayenne, the sugar, the soy sauce, and the garlic paste, add the beef, tossing it to coat it well, and let it marinate for 15 minutes.

In a large skillet heat 1 tablespoon of the oil over moderately high heat until it is hot but not smoking, in it stir-fry the beef for 2 minutes, or just until it is still pink, and transfer the beef to a bowl.

In the skillet heat the remaining 1 tablespoon oil until it is hot but not smoking and in it stir-fry the bean sprouts and the onion for 30 seconds, or until they are just wilted. Transfer the bean sprout mixture to the bowl, add the coriander, and toss the ingredients to combine them well. Divide the mixture between 2 plates, lined with the lettuce leaves, and garnish the salads with the lime wedges. Serves 2.

Vegetable Salads

Green and Black Bean Salad with Hard-Boiled Egg

¼ pound green beans, trimmed and cut
  into ½-inch pieces
2 tablespoons fresh lemon juice
¼ teaspoon dried hot red pepper flakes,
  or to taste
¼ cup olive oil
a 1-pound can black beans, drained, blanched
  in boiling water for 5 seconds, and
  drained well
½ cup chopped scallion
½ cup chopped celery
2 cups shredded romaine, rinsed, spun dry,
  and chilled
2 hard-boiled large eggs, chopped

In a saucepan of boiling salted water blanch the green beans for 3 to 5 minutes, or until they are just tender, drain them in a colander, and refresh them under cold water. Drain the beans well.

In a bowl whisk together the lemon juice, the red pepper flakes, and salt to taste, add the oil in a stream, whisking, and whisk the dressing until it is emulsified. Add the green beans, the black beans, the scallion, the celery, and salt and pepper to taste and toss the mixture to coat it with the dressing. Divide the romaine between chilled plates, top it with the bean salad, and sprinkle each salad with half of the chopped eggs. Serves 2.

Green Bean, Swiss Cheese, and Hazelnut Salad

½ **pound green beans, trimmed**
½ **cup julienne strips of Swiss cheese (about 2 ounces)**
¼ **cup chopped hazelnuts, lightly toasted and skin rubbed off**
2 **tablespoons olive oil**
1 **tablespoon fresh lemon juice**
1 **tablespoon minced fresh parsley leaves**
1 **small garlic clove, minced and mashed to a paste with ¼ teaspoon salt if desired**

In a saucepan of boiling salted water cook the green beans for 5 to 7 minutes, or until they are just tender. Drain the beans in a colander, refresh them under cold water, and pat them dry. In a bowl toss the beans with the cheese, the hazelnuts, and the oil until they are coated with the oil, add the lemon juice, the parsley, the garlic, and salt and pepper to taste, and toss the mixture well. Serves 2.

Carrot Salad in Zucchini Boats

two 6-inch zucchini
¼ **cup olive oil**
¾ **pound carrots, grated fine**
¼ **cup fresh lemon juice**
2 **teaspoons snipped fresh dill or ¾ teaspoon dried, crumbled**
freshly ground white pepper to taste
fresh dill sprigs and cherry tomatoes for garnish

Halve the zucchini lengthwise and scoop out and discard the pulp, leaving ¼-inch shells. In a skillet cook the zucchini shells cut sides up in 1 tablespoon of the oil, covered, over moderately high heat for 3 to 4 minutes, or until they are just tender. Sprinkle the shells lightly with salt, invert them onto paper towels, and let them drain for 15 minutes.

In another skillet cook the carrots in the remaining 3 tablespoons oil with the lemon juice over moderately high heat, stirring, for 3 minutes, or until the liquid is evaporated, and transfer the carrots to a metal bowl. Let the carrots cool, tossing them occasionally, add the snipped dill, the white pepper, and salt to taste, and toss the salad. Pat the zucchini shells dry, mound the carrot salad in them, and arrange the zucchini boats on a platter. Garnish the platter with the dill sprigs and the cherry tomatoes. Serves 2.

Carrots with Spinach Yogurt Sauce

5 **ounces spinach, washed and stems discarded**
½ **cup plain yogurt at room temperature**
¼ **teaspoon ground cumin**
½ **pound carrots, cut into 3- by ¼-inch sticks**

In a saucepan steam the spinach in the water clinging to the leaves, covered, over moderate heat for 2 to 3 minutes, or until it is wilted. In a blender purée the spinach with the liquid remaining in the pan, return the purée to the pan, and whisk in the yogurt, the cumin, and salt to taste. Keep the sauce warm, covered, over low heat, but do not let it boil.

In a saucepan cook the carrots in boiling salted water to cover for 5 to 8 minutes, or until they are just tender, drain them, and transfer them to heated plates. Spoon the sauce around the carrots. Serves 2 as a salad or first course.

Lentil Salad

½ cup lentils, picked over and rinsed
3 tablespoons minced onion
3 tablespoons minced carrot
1 teaspoon minced fresh parsley leaves
¼ teaspoon minced garlic
¼ teaspoon dried thyme, crumbled
½ bay leaf
½ teaspoon salt
2¼ cups water
1 tablespoon drained capers, chopped
⅔ cup herbed French dressing (recipe follows)
lettuce leaves for lining the platter
toast points as an accompaniment

In a saucepan combine the lentils, the onion, the carrot, the parsley, the garlic, the thyme, the bay leaf, the salt, pepper to taste, and the water, bring the water to a boil, and simmer the mixture, covered, for 18 minutes, or until the lentils are just tender. Drain the mixture in a sieve, discard the bay leaf, and chill the lentils in a metal bowl, covered, for 10 minutes. Whisk the capers into the dressing, toss the lentils with the dressing, and transfer the salad to a platter lined with the lettuce. Serve the salad with the toast points. Serves 2.

164

Herbed French Dressing

2 tablespoons wine vinegar
½ teaspoon Dijon-style mustard
⅓ to ½ cup olive oil, or to taste
1½ teaspoons minced fresh parsley leaves
1½ teaspoons snipped fresh chives
1½ teaspoons minced fresh tarragon
1½ teaspoons minced fresh chervil or
    ½ teaspoon dried, crumbled

In a bowl combine the vinegar, the mustard, and salt and pepper to taste, add the oil in a stream, whisking, and whisk the dressing until it is emulsified. Stir in the parsley, the chives, the tarragon, and the chervil. Makes about ⅔ cup.

Snow Pea and Green Bean Salad

1 tablespoon white-wine vinegar
3 tablespoons olive oil
½ pound green beans, trimmed
¼ pound snow peas, trimmed and strings
    discarded
2 tablespoons shelled sunflower seeds,
    toasted lightly

In a small bowl whisk together the vinegar, the oil, and salt and pepper to taste. In a large saucepan of boiling salted water cook the green beans for 4 minutes, or until they are just crisp-tender, add the snow peas, and cook the vegetables for 10 seconds. Drain the vegetables, transfer them to a bowl of ice and cold water to stop the cooking, and drain them. Pat the vegetables dry between several thicknesses of paper towels and in a bowl toss them with the sunflower seeds and the dressing. Serves 2.

Photo on page 30

Tomato, Cucumber, and Feta Salad

1 teaspoon red-wine vinegar
¼ teaspoon sugar
1 tablespoon olive oil
1½ cups quartered cherry tomatoes
1 small cucumber, peeled, halved lengthwise,
  seeded, and cut crosswise into ¼-inch slices
½ cup crumbled Feta
¼ cup shredded fresh basil leaves

In a bowl whisk together the vinegar, the sugar, the oil, and salt and pepper to taste, add the tomatoes, the cucumber, the Feta, and the basil, and toss the salad well. Serves 2.

Photo on page 68

Chopped Vegetable Salad with Feta

1 tablespoon red-wine vinegar
½ teaspoon Dijon-style mustard
2 tablespoons olive oil
1 cup chopped broccoli
1 large carrot, grated coarse
⅓ cup chopped fennel bulb (sometimes called
  anise, available in most supermarkets)
3 tablespoons chopped or crumbled Feta

In a small bowl whisk together the vinegar, the mustard, and salt to taste, add the oil in a stream, whisking, and whisk the dressing until it is emulsified. In a small saucepan cook the broccoli in boiling salted water for 1½ minutes, or until it is crisp-tender, drain it in a colander, and refresh it under cold water. Pat the broccoli dry. Transfer the broccoli to a bowl, add the carrot, the fennel, the Feta, the dressing, and salt and pepper to taste, and toss the salad well. Serves 2.

Pasta and Grain Salads
❦ ❦ ❦

Pasta with Bell Peppers, Goat Cheese, and Basil

2 garlic cloves, minced
2 tablespoons olive oil
½ cup finely chopped onion
1 large red bell pepper, cut into julienne strips
  (about 1 cup)
1 large yellow bell pepper, cut into julienne
  strips (about 1 cup)
⅓ cup dry white wine or dry vermouth
⅓ cup sliced pitted Kalamata or other
  brine-cured black olives
½ cup finely shredded fresh basil leaves
½ pound *rotelle* or *fusilli*
3 ounces mild goat cheese such as
  Montrachet, crumbled (about 1 cup)

In a skillet cook the garlic in the oil over moderately low heat, stirring, for 1 minute, add the onion, and cook the mixture, stirring, until the onion is softened. Add the bell peppers, cook the mixture over moderate heat, stirring, for 5 minutes, or until the peppers are just tender, and add the wine and the olives. Boil the wine until it is reduced by half, season the mixture with salt and pepper to taste, and stir in the basil. In a kettle of boiling salted water cook the pasta for 8 to 10 minutes, or until it is *al dente* and drain it well, reserving ⅓ cup of the cooking water. In a serving bowl whisk two thirds of the goat cheese with the reserved cooking water until the cheese is melted and the mixture is smooth, add the pasta and the bell pepper mixture, and toss the mixture well. Sprinkle the pasta with the remaining goat cheese. Serves 2.

Photo on page 22

165

Rice and Pine Nut Salad

1 tablespoon unsalted butter
½ teaspoon salt
1⅓ cups water
⅔ cup long-grain rice
¼ cup minced fresh parsley leaves
¼ cup minced red bell pepper
¼ cup pine nuts, toasted lightly
2 tablespoons fresh lime juice
2 tablespoons olive oil
lettuce leaves for lining the platter

In a saucepan combine the butter and the salt with the water, bring the water to a boil, and stir in the rice. Simmer the rice, covered, for 20 minutes, or until it is tender and the liquid is absorbed, transfer it to a metal bowl, and let it cool, tossing it occasionally. Stir in the parsley, the bell pepper, and the pine nuts.

In a bowl combine the lime juice and salt to taste, add the oil in a stream, whisking, and whisk the dressing until it is emulsified. Toss the rice mixture with the dressing and transfer the salad to a platter lined with the lettuce. Serves 2.

Tortellini Salad with Arugula

1 teaspoon Dijon-style mustard
2 tablespoons red-wine vinegar
⅓ cup olive oil
½ zucchini, scored lengthwise with the tines of a fork, quartered lengthwise, and cut crosswise into ¼-inch slices
9 ounces fresh *tortellini*
1 small red bell pepper, cut into ½- by ⅛-inch pieces
2 tablespoons freshly grated Parmesan
2 tablespoons minced fresh parsley leaves
4 cups loosely packed *arugula* or watercress, coarse stems discarded, rinsed well and spun dry

In a small bowl whisk together the mustard, the vinegar, and salt to taste, add the oil in a stream, whisking, and whisk the dressing until it is emulsified. In a saucepan of boiling salted water blanch the zucchini for 1 minute, or until it just begins to turn translucent, drain it, and refresh it in a bowl of ice and cold water. In a large saucepan cook the *tortellini* in boiling salted water for 5 minutes, or until it is *al dente*, drain it in a colander, and refresh it under cold water. Drain the zucchini and the *tortellini* well and in a bowl combine them with the bell pepper, the Parmesan, the parsley, three fourths of the dressing, and salt and pepper to taste, tossing the ingredients well to coat them with the dressing. In another bowl toss the *arugula* with the remaining dressing and divide it and the *tortellini* between 2 plates. Serves 2.

Photo on page 167

Tortellini Salad with Arugula

Dirty Rice Dressing

½ cup long-grain rice
½ pound ground beef
½ pound ground pork
2 ounces chicken livers, chopped fine
2 ounces chicken gizzards, chopped fine
⅔ cup minced green bell pepper
1 small onion, minced
1 large garlic clove, minced
¼ cup minced fresh parsley leaves
½ cup chopped scallion greens
cayenne to taste

In a saucepan bring 1 cup salted water to a boil, stir in the rice, and simmer it, covered, for 20 minutes, or until it is tender and the water is absorbed.

In a large heavy skillet sauté the beef and the pork over moderately high heat, stirring, for 5 to 8 minutes, or until the meat is well browned, stir in the liver, the gizzards, the bell pepper, the onion, and the garlic, and cook the mixture over moderate heat, stirring occasionally, until the vegetables are softened. Add ½ cup water and cook the mixture, covered, until the liquid is absorbed. Stir in 1 cup water and cook the mixture, covered, over moderately low heat for 15 minutes. Remove the skillet from the heat and stir in the parsley, the scallion greens, the cayenne, and salt to taste. In a bowl combine well the rice and the meat mixture and transfer the dressing to a heated serving dish. *Any leftover dirty rice dressing may be kept, covered and chilled, for 1 day.* Makes about 4 cups.

Green Salads and Slaws
❦ ❦ ❦

Herbed Boston Lettuce and Cherry Tomato Salad

2 to 3 teaspoons white-wine vinegar
2 tablespoons olive oil
3 cups shredded, washed, and spun-dry
   Boston lettuce (about 1 small head)
1 cup yellow or red cherry tomatoes,
   quartered
¼ cup packed fresh basil leaves, chopped fine
¼ cup loosely packed fresh parsley leaves,
   chopped fine
1 tablespoon chopped fresh chives

In a bowl whisk together the vinegar to taste, the oil, and salt and pepper to taste, whisking until the vinaigrette is emulsified. Add the lettuce, the tomatoes, the basil, the parsley, and the chives and toss the salad until it is combined well. Serves 2.

Photo on page 16

Escarole Salad with Honey Lime Dressing

1 teaspoon onion juice, made by pressing
   2 tablespoons chopped onion through a
   garlic press and straining the juice
1 teaspoon Dijon-style mustard
1 teaspoon fresh lime juice
½ teaspoon honey
2 tablespoons olive oil
4 cups loosely packed torn escarole leaves,
   rinsed and spun dry
1 hard-boiled egg, sieved

In a small bowl whisk together the onion juice, the mustard, the lime juice, the honey, and salt and pepper to taste, whisk in the oil, and whisk the dressing until it is emulsified. In a bowl toss the escarole with the dressing until it is coated well, divide the salad between 2 salad plates, and sprinkle it with the sieved egg. Serves 2.

Chef's Salads with Blue Cheese French Dressing

½ pound spinach, trimmed, washed,
   and patted dry
1 cucumber, peeled and sliced crosswise
¼ cup minced scallion
½ cup blue cheese French dressing
   (recipe follows)
2 ounces salami, sliced thin and cut into
   triangles
3 ounces Havarti, sliced thin and cut into
   ½-inch squares
2 hard-boiled large eggs, quartered
freshly ground pepper to taste

In a large bowl toss the spinach, the cucumber, and 2 tablespoons of the scallion with ¼ cup of the dressing. Divide the spinach mixture between 2 bowls, arrange the salami, the Havarti, and the eggs on it, and add the pepper. Sprinkle the salads with the remaining 2 tablespoons scallion and serve the remaining ¼ cup dressing separately. Serves 2.

Blue Cheese French Dressing

2 tablespoons wine vinegar
¼ cup olive oil
1 tablespoon heavy cream
2 tablespoons crumbled blue cheese
a few drops of fresh lemon juice

In a bowl combine the vinegar with salt and pepper to taste, add the oil and the cream in a stream, whisking, and whisk the dressing until it is emulsified. Stir in the blue cheese and the lemon juice. Makes about ½ cup.

Watercress, Endive, and Goat Cheese Salad

enough Italian bread cut into ½-inch cubes to measure 1 cup
¼ cup olive oil
1½ tablespoons fresh lemon juice, or to taste
½ teaspoon Dijon-style mustard
1 teaspoon minced fresh thyme leaves or ¼ teaspoon dried, crumbled
3 cups loosely packed watercress, coarse stems discarded, rinsed well, and spun dry
1 small Belgian endive, trimmed and sliced thin crosswise
2 ounces mild goat cheese such as Montrachet, crumbled (about ½ cup)

In a bowl toss the bread cubes with 1 tablespoon of the oil and salt to taste and on a baking sheet toast them in the middle of a preheated 350° F. oven for 10 minutes, or until they are golden. Transfer the croutons to a salad bowl and let them cool. In another small bowl whisk together the lemon juice, the mustard, the thyme, and salt and pepper to taste, add the remaining 3 tablespoons oil in a stream, whisking, and whisk the dressing until it is emulsified. To the croutons add the watercress, the endive, the goat cheese, and the dressing and toss the salad well. Serves 2.

Napa Coleslaw with Dill

3 cups thinly sliced Napa cabbage (about ¾ pound)
1 carrot, grated
1 tablespoon minced fresh dill
¼ teaspoon sugar
¼ teaspoon salt
2 tablespoons olive oil
2 teaspoons red-wine vinegar, or to taste

In a bowl combine the cabbage, the carrot, and the dill. Sprinkle the mixture with the sugar, the salt, and the oil, tossing it to combine it well, and sprinkle the coleslaw with the vinegar, tossing it to combine it well. Serves 2.

Red Cabbage and Green Apple Coleslaw

3 tablespoons mayonnaise
3 tablespoons plain yogurt
1½ teaspoons red-wine vinegar
1 teaspoon Dijon-style mustard
½ teaspoon sugar
2½ cups finely shredded red cabbage
1 Granny Smith apple, peeled if desired and grated coarse

In a bowl whisk together the mayonnaise, the yogurt, the vinegar, the mustard, the sugar, and salt and pepper to taste. Add the cabbage and the apple to the dressing and toss the coleslaw until it is combined well. Serves 2.

Apple Ginger Upside-Down Cake

DESSERTS

A h… desserts! Whether it's a simple cobbler or a spectacular mousse, no other part of the meal is so sure to please your guests. Here you will find shortcuts to classic favorites and many other lovely surprises.

Most people relish a piece of apple pie now and then, but how often do you have the time to bake one? Our delicious individual Apple Tarts eliminate the need to make fresh dough and boast light flaky crusts made from frozen puff pastry instead. You are sure to receive rave reviews *and* you will save half the time. For chocoholics we have a wonderful temptation in store. Our Chocolate Raspberry Shortcakes combine dark, rich, and tender biscuits with fresh, sweet raspberries and whipped cream—a delicious and very memorable splurge. Once you try these you will be looking forward to raspberry season every year.

Fruit crisps, tea cakes, puddings, cookies—they are all here. But, for those evenings when baking is not an option, remember good ol' vanilla ice cream. You can easily add a little embellishment to make it become the dessert you need. Our Gingered Rhubarb with Vanilla Ice Cream, for example, is an exotic treat that can be made in minutes. On the other hand, our down-home Peach, Pecan, and Rum Caramel Sundaes are hard to beat. Take your pick and enjoy!

Cakes
❧ ❧ ❧

Apple Ginger Upside-Down Cake

½ stick (¼ cup) unsalted butter, melted
¼ cup firmly packed light brown sugar
2 tablespoons finely chopped crystallized
   ginger plus additional for garnish
2 tablespoons currants or raisins
1 large McIntosh or Granny Smith apple,
   peeled, cored, and sliced thin
1 tablespoon fresh lemon juice
½ cup all-purpose flour
½ teaspoon double-acting baking powder
¼ teaspoon salt
½ teaspoon cinnamon
2 large eggs
¼ cup plus 2 tablespoons granulated sugar
½ teaspoon vanilla
whipped cream or vanilla ice cream as an
   accompaniment

Into an 8-inch round cake pan pour the butter, swirling the pan, and sprinkle it with the brown sugar, 2 tablespoons of the ginger, and the currants. In a small bowl toss the apple slices with the lemon juice and arrange them evenly over the currants. Into another bowl sift together the flour, the baking powder, the salt, and the cinnamon. In a bowl with an electric mixer beat the eggs with the granulated sugar and the vanilla for 3 to 5 minutes, or until the mixture is thick and pale and forms a ribbon when the beaters are lifted. Fold in the flour mixture gently but thoroughly, pour the batter over the apple slices, and bake the cake in the middle of a preheated 400° F. oven for 20 to 25 minutes, or until a tester comes out clean. Run a sharp knife around the edge of the pan, invert the cake onto a serving plate, and serve it warm with the whipped cream, sprinkled with the additional ginger. Makes one 8-inch cake.

Photo on page 170

Warm Upside-Down Cheesecakes with Blueberry Sauce

1 tablespoon unsalted butter
¼ cup graham cracker crumbs
¾ cup cream cheese, softened
¼ cup plus 2 tablespoons sugar
¼ teaspoon vanilla
¼ teaspoon almond extract
1 large egg
1 cup blueberries, picked over
⅓ cup water
2 teaspoons cornstarch dissolved in
   1 tablespoon water
fresh lemon juice to taste

In a small saucepan melt the butter over moderate heat, stir in the crumbs, and divide the mixture among four paper-lined ½-cup muffin tins, patting the mixture to form a crust. Bake the crusts in the middle of a preheated 350° F. oven for 5 minutes, and let them cool on a rack for 5 minutes.

In a bowl with an electric mixer beat together the cream cheese, ¼ cup of the sugar, the vanilla, the almond extract, and a pinch of salt until the mixture is combined well, beat in the egg, beating until the batter is combined well, and divide the batter among the tins. (The batter will fill the tins.) Bake the cheesecakes in the middle of a preheated 350° F. oven for 20 minutes, or until they are set, and let them cool on a rack for 10 minutes.

While the cheesecakes are baking, in a small heavy saucepan combine the blueberries, the remaining 2 tablespoons sugar, and the water, bring the mixture to a boil, and simmer it, stirring occasionally, for 3 minutes. Stir the cornstarch mixture, add it to the blueberries with the lemon juice, and simmer the mixture, stirring, for 2 minutes.

Discard the paper liners, invert the cheesecakes onto plates, and spoon the sauce around them. Makes 4 individual cheesecakes, serving 2.

Chocolate Raspberry Shortcakes

For the shortcakes
2 tablespoons unsweetened cocoa powder
½ cup all-purpose flour
2 tablespoons granulated sugar
¾ teaspoon double-acting baking powder
¼ teaspoon baking soda
⅛ teaspoon salt
2 tablespoons cold unsalted butter, cut
   into bits
4 tablespoons heavy cream

1½ cups raspberries
2 tablespoons granulated sugar, or to taste
1 tablespoon framboise, or to taste
⅓ cup well-chilled heavy cream
confectioners' sugar for sprinkling the
   shortcakes
mint sprigs for garnish if desired

Make the shortcakes: Into a bowl sift together the cocoa powder, the flour, the sugar, the baking powder, the baking soda, and the salt, add the butter, and blend the mixture until it resembles coarse meal. Add the cream and stir the mixture with a fork until it forms a dough. Divide the dough in half, arrange each half in a mound on a lightly greased baking sheet, and bake the shortcakes in the middle of a preheated 425° F. oven for 12 minutes, or until a tester inserted in the centers comes out with crumbs clinging to it. Transfer the shortcakes to a rack and let them cool.

In a small bowl mash ¾ cup of the raspberries with a fork, stir in 1 tablespoon of the granulated sugar and the framboise, stirring until the sugar is dissolved, and stir in the remaining ¾ cup raspberries. In a small bowl with an electric mixer beat the cream until it holds soft peaks, add the remaining 1 tablespoon granulated sugar, and beat the cream until it holds stiff peaks. Carefully cut the shortcakes in half horizontally with a serrated knife and with a metal spatula transfer the bottom half of each to an individual plate. (The shortcakes are delicate and crumble easily.) Top each bottom half with half the raspberry mixture, divide the whipped cream between the 2 shortcakes, and with the spatula carefully top each serving with the top half of a shortcake. Sprinkle the shortcakes with the confectioners' sugar and garnish the plates with the mint sprigs. Serves 2.

Photo on page 2

Almond Tea Cakes

¾ cup confectioners' sugar, sifted
½ cup whole natural almonds, toasted lightly
   and ground fine
2½ tablespoons all-purpose flour
¾ stick (6 tablespoons) unsalted butter
⅓ cup egg whites (about 3 large eggs)
1 tablespoon rum

In a bowl stir together the sugar, the almonds, and the flour until the mixture is combined well. In a skillet melt the butter over moderately high heat and cook it, swirling the skillet occasionally, until the foam subsides and the butter is light brown. Stir the egg whites and the rum gently into the almond mixture until the mixture is just combined and stir in the hot butter. Divide the batter between nine ¼-cup buttered muffin cups and bake the cakes in a preheated 450° F. oven for 6 minutes. Lower the heat to 400° F., bake the cakes for 6 minutes more, and turn the oven off, leaving the cakes in it for 10 minutes more. Transfer the cakes immediately to racks and let them cool. Makes 9 tea cakes.

Lemon Poppy Seed Tea Cakes

⅔ cup cake flour (not self-rising)
¼ teaspoon baking soda
½ stick (¼ cup) unsalted butter, softened
⅔ cup granulated sugar
2 large eggs, separated
1½ tablespoons fresh lemon juice
1 teaspoon vanilla
1½ teaspoons freshly grated lemon zest
2½ tablespoons poppy seeds
¼ cup sour cream
confectioners' sugar for dusting the cakes

Into a bowl sift together the flour, the baking soda, and a pinch of salt. In a large bowl with an electric mixer cream the butter, add ⅓ cup of the granulated sugar, a little at a time, beating, and beat the mixture until it is light and fluffy. Add the egg yolks, 1 at a time, beating

well after each addition, and beat in well the lemon juice, the vanilla, the zest, and the poppy seeds. Add the flour mixture to the butter mixture alternately with the sour cream, combining the mixture well.

In another large bowl with the electric mixer beat the egg whites until they hold soft peaks, beat in the remaining ⅓ cup granulated sugar, a little at a time, and beat the meringue until it holds stiff peaks. Stir one fourth of the meringue into the cake batter and fold in the remaining meringue gently but thoroughly.

Divide the batter among 6 well-buttered and floured ½-cup muffin tins and bake the tea cakes in the middle of a preheated 375° F. oven for 20 to 25 minutes, or until they are golden. Turn the tea cakes out onto a rack and sift the confectioners' sugar over the tops. Makes 6 tea cakes.

Photo on this page

Lemon Poppy Seed Tea Cakes

Whipped Cream Cakes with Strawberry Sauce

¾ cup all-purpose flour
1 teaspoon double-acting baking powder
¼ teaspoon salt
1 large whole egg plus 1 large egg yolk
¼ teaspoon almond extract
½ cup granulated sugar
⅔ cup well-chilled heavy cream

For the strawberry sauce
1½ cups strawberries
3 tablespoons granulated sugar

confectioners' sugar for dusting the cakes

Into a bowl sift together the flour, the baking powder, and the salt. In a bowl with an electric mixer beat together the whole egg and the additional yolk, the almond extract, and ¼ cup of the granulated sugar until the mixture is thick and pale. In another bowl beat the cream with the cleaned beaters, adding the remaining ¼ cup granulated sugar, until the mixture holds soft peaks. Fold the egg mixture into the whipped cream mixture and fold the flour mixture into the cream mixture.

Divide the cake batter among 9 paper-lined ½-cup muffin tins and bake the cakes in the middle of a preheated 350° F. oven for 18 to 20 minutes, or until a tester comes out clean. Let the cakes cool in the tins on a rack for 10 minutes, turn them out onto the rack, and remove the paper liners.

Meanwhile, make the strawberry sauce: In a blender purée the strawberries with the sugar and transfer the sauce to a bowl. Dust the cakes with the confectioners' sugar and serve them with the strawberry sauce. Makes 9 individual cakes.

Peanut Brownie Torte

1 cup (6 ounces) semisweet chocolate chips
2 tablespoons smooth peanut butter
1 tablespoon unsalted butter
1 large egg
¼ cup sugar
½ teaspoon vanilla
2 tablespoons all-purpose flour
½ cup chopped unsalted dry-roasted peanuts
vanilla ice cream as an accompaniment

Butter and flour an 8-inch round cake pan. In a small metal bowl set over barely simmering water melt ¾ cup of the chocolate chips, the peanut butter, and the butter, stirring until the mixture is smooth. In a bowl whisk together the egg, the sugar, and the vanilla until the mixture is foamy, whisk in the chocolate mixture and a pinch of salt, whisking until the mixture is smooth, and fold in the flour, the remaining ¼ cup chocolate chips, and the peanuts. Spoon the batter into the pan, spreading it evenly, and bake the torte in the middle of a preheated 350° F. oven for 15 to 20 minutes, or until a tester comes out with some crumbs adhering to it. Transfer the torte to a rack, let it cool for 10 minutes, and serve it warm, cut into wedges, with the ice cream. Makes one 8-inch torte.

Fruit Desserts
🍎 🍎 🍎

Apple Pecan Shortbread Tarts

⅓ cup all-purpose flour
1 tablespoon cornstarch
1 tablespoon superfine sugar
½ stick (¼ cup) unsalted butter, softened
3 tablespoons pecans, toasted lightly and
   chopped fine
1 tart apple, peeled and cut lengthwise into
   ¼-inch slices
¼ cup granulated sugar
¼ cup heavy cream

In a small bowl combine the flour, the corn-starch, and the superfine sugar, blend in 3 tablespoons of the butter until the mixture resembles coarse meal, and stir in the pecans. Halve the dough, press it into 2 well-buttered 4½-inch fluted tart pans, and bake the short-bread in a preheated 350° F. oven for 15 to 20 minutes, or until it is golden.

In a skillet melt the remaining 1 table-spoon butter over moderate heat and in it cook the apple slices, turning them once, for 8 to 10 minutes, or until they are golden and tender. In a heavy saucepan combine the gran-ulated sugar and the cream and boil the mix-ture gently, stirring occasionally, for 8 to 10 minutes, or until it thickens. Arrange the apple slices on the shortbread and spoon the sauce over them. Serves 2.

Apple Tarts

1 sheet (½ pound) frozen puff pastry,
   thawed
1 large Granny Smith apple
2 tablespoons sugar
¼ teaspoon cinnamon
1 tablespoon cold unsalted butter,
   cut into bits
2 tablespoons apricot jam, heated and
   strained
vanilla ice cream or whipped cream as an
   accompaniment

Roll out the pastry ⅛ inch thick on a lightly floured surface, cut out two 7-inch rounds, and transfer them to a baking sheet. Peel, halve lengthwise, and core the apple, slice it thin crosswise, and arrange the slices, overlap-ping them slightly, on the pastry rounds. In a small bowl stir together the sugar and the cin-namon, sprinkle the mixture evenly over the apple slices, and dot the tarts with the butter. Bake the tarts in the middle of a preheated 400° F. oven for 25 minutes, or until the pas-try is golden brown. (If doubling the recipe and using 2 baking sheets, alternate the sheets on the middle and upper-third racks of the oven halfway through the baking time.) Transfer the tarts to a rack, brush them with the jam, and serve them warm with the ice cream. Serves 2.

Photo on page 20

Apricot Pine Nut Crisp

2 tablespoons unsalted butter
1½ teaspoons honey
¼ cup all-purpose flour
2 tablespoons firmly packed dark brown sugar
2 tablespoons chopped lightly toasted
  pine nuts
6 apricots (about 1 pound)
vanilla ice cream as an accompaniment
  if desired

In a small saucepan heat the butter and the honey over low heat, stirring, until the butter is melted. In a bowl combine well the flour and the brown sugar, add the butter mixture, stirring, and stir the mixture until it is combined well. Stir in the pine nuts. Cut the apricots, peeled, into ¼-inch slices and layer the slices in a 2½- to 3-cup shallow baking dish. Crumble the pine nut topping over the apricots and bake the crisp in a preheated 400° F. oven for 15 to 20 minutes, or until the top is golden brown and the apricots are tender. Serve the crisp warm with the ice cream if desired. Serves 2.

Gingered Poached Apricot and Raspberry Compote

⅓ cup sugar
⅓ cup water
1½ tablespoons fresh lemon juice, or to taste
2 teaspoons fine julienne strips of peeled
  fresh gingerroot
3 fresh apricots, quartered
½ cup raspberries
1 tablespoon sliced almonds, toasted lightly
mint sprigs for garnish

In a small saucepan stir together the sugar, the water, the lemon juice, and the gingerroot and simmer the mixture, covered, for 5 minutes. Add the apricots, baste them with the syrup, and poach them, covered, over moderately low heat for 3 minutes, or until they are just tender. Stir in the raspberries gently, poach the mixture for 1 minute, and divide it between 2 bowls. Sprinkle the compote with the almonds, garnish it with the mint, and serve it warm or at room temperature. Serves 2.

Photo on page 28

Sautéed Bananas with Maple Praline Sauce

½ cup maple syrup
¼ cup heavy cream
¼ cup chopped pecans
2 bananas, peeled and halved lengthwise and
  then crosswise
2 tablespoons unsalted butter
vanilla ice cream as an accompaniment
  if desired

In a saucepan combine the maple syrup, the cream, and the pecans, bring the liquid to a gentle boil over moderate heat, and cook the mixture, stirring occasionally, for 18 to 20 minutes, or until it is thickened. In a skillet sauté the bananas in the butter over moderately high heat for 1 to 2 minutes on each side, or until they are browned lightly. Transfer the bananas to a heated platter and spoon the sauce over them or, if desired, use the bananas and the sauce as a topping for the ice cream. Serves 2.

Chocolate Sponge Moons Filled with Peaches and Cream

Cranberry Pear Cobbler

1½ cups cranberries, picked over
1 pear, peeled, cored, and sliced thin
1½ teaspoons freshly grated orange zest
½ cup firmly packed light brown sugar
¼ teaspoon cardamom
a pinch of ground ginger
½ cup plus 1 tablespoon all-purpose flour
1 tablespoon unsalted butter, cut into bits
½ teaspoon double-acting baking powder
¼ teaspoon salt
2 tablespoons vegetable shortening
¼ cup milk
½ teaspoon granulated sugar
vanilla ice cream as an accompaniment
 if desired

In a bowl toss together the cranberries, the pear, the zest, the brown sugar, the cardamom, the ginger, and 1 tablespoon of the flour, transfer the mixture to a shallow 2-cup baking dish, and dot the top with the butter. In a bowl stir together the remaining ½ cup flour, the baking powder, and the salt. Add the shortening, blend the mixture until it resembles coarse meal, and stir in the milk. (The dough will be sticky.) Drop the dough by spoonfuls onto the cranberry mixture, sprinkle it with the granulated sugar, and bake the cobbler in the middle of a preheated 400° F. oven for 30 minutes, or until the top is golden. Serve the cobbler with the ice cream. Serves 2.

Chocolate Sponge Moons Filled with Peaches and Cream

For the sponge moons
2 large egg whites
5 tablespoons granulated sugar
2 large egg yolks
¼ cup unsweetened cocoa powder
2 tablespoons all-purpose flour
⅛ teaspoon salt

For the filling
½ cup well-chilled heavy cream
1 tablespoon peach schnapps if desired
½ ounce unsweetened chocolate, grated
1 large peach, halved lengthwise, pitted,
    cut into 12 slices, and sprinkled with fresh
    lemon juice, reserving 4 slices for garnish

For the sauce
½ peach, the cut side sprinkled with fresh
    lemon juice
2 tablespoons fresh lemon juice
2 tablespoons water
2 tablespoons granulated sugar

confectioners' sugar for dusting the desserts
2 mint sprigs for garnish if desired

Make the sponge moons: Line a buttered baking sheet with a piece of parchment paper or foil and butter the paper. In a small bowl with an electric mixer beat the egg whites with a pinch of salt until they are foamy, add gradually 3 tablespoons of the sugar, beating, and beat the whites until they just hold stiff peaks. In another bowl whisk together the egg yolks and the remaining 2 tablespoons sugar until the mixture is combined well. Fold the whites into the yolk mixture, sift together the cocoa powder, the flour, and the salt over the mixture, and fold the mixture together gently but thoroughly. Divide the mixture into 2 mounds spaced well apart on the prepared baking sheet and with a rubber spatula spread the mounds carefully, forming two 6-inch rounds. Bake the

rounds in a preheated 400° F. oven for 5 minutes, or until they are springy to the touch, let them cool on the baking sheet for 5 minutes, and transfer them with a metal spatula to a rack. While they are still warm drape the sponge rounds over a rolling pin suspended between 2 inverted mugs and let them cool completely.

Make the filling while the sponge moons are cooling: In a well-chilled bowl with an electric mixer beat the cream, with the schnapps if desired, until the mixture just holds stiff peaks, fold in the chocolate, and transfer the mixture to a pastry bag fitted with a large star tip. Put each sponge moon on a dessert plate, arrange 4 peach slices inside each one, and pipe the flavored whipped cream decoratively over the peaches. (Alternatively, the whipped cream may be spooned over the peaches.)

Make the sauce: In a blender purée the half peach, peeled and pitted, with the lemon juice, the water, and the sugar and spoon half the sauce on each plate.

Dust the filled moons with the confectioners' sugar and garnish each dessert with 2 of the reserved peach slices and a mint sprig if desired. Serves 2.

Photo on page 178

Lemon Yogurt Mousse

1¼ teaspoons unflavored gelatin
¼ cup fresh lemon juice
⅓ cup sugar
1 teaspoon freshly grated lemon zest
1 tablespoon unsalted butter
1 cup plain yogurt
lightly sweetened whipped cream as
 an accompaniment

In a small saucepan sprinkle the gelatin over the lemon juice and let it soften for 1 minute. Add the sugar, the zest, and the butter and heat the mixture over moderate heat, stirring, until the gelatin is dissolved. Transfer the mixture to a metal bowl set in a larger bowl of ice and cold water and stir the mixture until it is the consistency of raw egg white. Whisk the yogurt into the lemon mixture, divide the mousse between 2 serving glasses, and chill it for 30 minutes. Serve the mousse topped with the whipped cream. Serves 2.

Nectarine Crisp

¼ teaspoon freshly grated orange zest
1 tablespoon fresh orange juice
2 teaspoons sugar
½ teaspoon cornstarch
1¾ cups peeled, pitted, chopped nectarines
 (about 2 nectarines)

For the topping
¼ cup firmly packed light brown sugar
¼ cup all-purpose flour
3 tablespoons old-fashioned rolled oats
¼ teaspoon freshly grated nutmeg
⅛ teaspoon salt
2 tablespoons cold unsalted butter,
 cut into bits

sour cream as an accompaniment if desired

In a small bowl combine well the zest, the juice, the sugar, and the cornstarch and add the nectarines. Toss the nectarines to coat them with the orange mixture and transfer the mixture to a 7½-inch (2½-cup) shallow baking dish.

Make the topping: In another small bowl combine the brown sugar, the flour, the oats, the nutmeg, the salt, and the butter, blend the mixture until it resembles coarse meal, and sprinkle it evenly over the nectarine mixture.

Bake the nectarine crisp in a preheated 375° F. oven for 20 to 25 minutes, or until the nectarine mixture is bubbling around the edge of the dish and the top is golden. Let the nectarine crisp cool slightly and serve it with the sour cream if desired. Serves 2.

F r o z e n   D e s s e r t s

Bourbon Pineapple Coconut Ice Cream

¼ cup sweetened flaked coconut
½ tablespoon unsalted butter
2 tablespoons firmly packed light brown
 sugar
2 tablespoons water
¾ cup coarsely chopped pineapple
2 tablespoons bourbon
1½ cups slightly softened vanilla ice cream

In a small skillet sauté the coconut in the butter over moderately high heat, stirring, until it is golden and remove the pan from the heat. In a small saucepan stir together the brown sugar, the water, the pineapple, and the bourbon, bring the liquid to a boil, and simmer the mixture for 8 to 10 minutes, or until the liquid is reduced to about 1 teaspoon. Transfer the mixture to a metal bowl set over a bowl of ice and cold water and let it stand until it is cool. Add the softened ice cream and the coconut and with an electric mixer beat the mixture until it is combined well. Serves 2.

Gingered Rhubarb with Vanilla Ice Cream

Gingered Rhubarb with Vanilla Ice Cream

1¼ pounds rhubarb, trimmed and cut into
  ¾-inch pieces (about 3 cups)
3 tablespoons fresh orange juice
1 tablespoon minced peeled fresh gingerroot
⅓ cup sugar, or to taste
1 tablespoon unsalted butter
vanilla ice cream as an accompaniment
fresh mint sprigs for garnish

In a heavy saucepan combine the rhubarb, the orange juice, the gingerroot, and the sugar, cook the mixture over moderate heat, stirring occasionally, until the sugar is dissolved, and simmer it, covered, for 5 minutes, or until the rhubarb is tender. Add the butter, stirring until the butter is melted, and let the sauce cool slightly. Serve the sauce with the ice cream and garnish it with the mint. Makes about 2 cups, serving 2.

Photo on this page

Peach, Pecan, and Rum Caramel Sundaes

3 tablespoons unsalted butter
3 tablespoons chopped pecans
1 large peach (½ pound), peeled and chopped
2 tablespoons dark rum
2 firmly packed tablespoons light
   brown sugar
vanilla ice cream

In a skillet melt the butter over moderate heat until it is foamy and in it sauté the pecans over moderately high heat, stirring, for 15 seconds. Transfer the pecans with a slotted spoon to a small bowl and reserve them. In the skillet cook the peach pieces over moderate heat, stirring, until they are coated well with the butter, add the rum and the brown sugar, and bring the liquid to a boil. Simmer the peaches, swirling the skillet, until they are tender and the sauce is thickened, and stir in the reserved pecans. Serve the peach mixture over the ice cream. Serves 2.

Macadamia Mousse with Chocolate Rum Sauce

For the mousse
1 large egg
2 tablespoons sugar
⅓ cup unsalted macadamia nuts, chopped fine
¾ cup well-chilled heavy cream

For the chocolate rum sauce
¼ cup heavy cream
1 tablespoon dark rum
¼ cup semisweet chocolate chips

Make the mousse: In a metal bowl set over a saucepan of simmering water combine the egg and the sugar and with an electric mixer beat the mixture at high speed for 3 minutes, or

until it is thick and fluffy. Remove the pan from the heat and continue to beat the mixture set over the hot water for 3 minutes. Set the metal bowl in a bowl of ice and cold water, beat the mixture until it is cold, and stir in the macadamia nuts. In a chilled small bowl beat the cream with the electric mixer until it just holds stiff peaks, stir one fourth of the whipped cream into the macadamia mixture until it is combined well, and fold in the remaining whipped cream. Spoon the mousse into 2 chilled dessert glasses and chill it in the freezer for 25 minutes.

Make the chocolate rum sauce: In a small saucepan bring the cream and the rum to a boil, remove the pan from the heat, and add the chocolate chips. Whisk the mixture until the chocolate is melted and serve the warm sauce over the mousse. Serves 2.

Strawberry Italian Ice

1 pint fresh strawberries, trimmed
¼ cup sugar
2 teaspoons fresh lemon juice
2 cups ice cubes (about 11)

Put a 9- or 10-inch metal cake pan in the freezer. In a blender blend the strawberries, the sugar, and the lemon juice until the mixture is smooth and the sugar is dissolved. Add the ice cubes, blend the mixture until it is smooth, and pour it into the cold pan. Freeze the mixture for 30 to 40 minutes, or until it is frozen around the edge but still soft in the center, stir the strawberry ice, mashing the frozen parts with a fork, and spoon it into 2 bowls. Serves 2.

Other Desserts
❧ ❧ ❧

Molasses Pecan Sweet Bread

½ cup unsulfured molasses
¼ cup vegetable oil
½ cup hot water
½ cup sugar
1½ cups all-purpose flour
½ teaspoon baking soda
¼ teaspoon cinnamon
a pinch of ground ginger
a pinch of nutmeg
1 cup pecans, toasted lightly and chopped
whipped cream as an accompaniment

In a bowl with an electric mixer beat the molasses, the oil, and the hot water until the mixture is combined, add the sugar, beating, and beat the mixture until it is combined. Into another bowl sift together the flour, the baking soda, the cinnamon, the ginger, and the nutmeg. Add the flour mixture to the molasses mixture, a little at a time, beating, and beat the batter until it is combined well. Stir in the pecans, spoon the batter into a buttered and floured 8-inch-square cake pan, and bake the bread in a preheated 350° F. oven for 30 to 35 minutes, or until a tester comes out clean. Let the bread cool in the pan on a rack for 3 minutes, run a thin knife around the edges to loosen it, and turn the bread out onto the rack. Cut the bread into squares and serve it warm with the whipped cream. *The squares may be kept, wrapped and chilled, for up to 2 days.*

Ginger Chocolate Chip Cookies

1½ cups all-purpose flour
1 tablespoon ground ginger
½ teaspoon baking soda
1 large egg, beaten lightly
2 tablespoons honey
4 teaspoons milk
1½ teaspoons freshly grated orange zest
1½ sticks (¾ cup) unsalted butter, softened
½ cup firmly packed dark brown sugar
1 cup semisweet chocolate chips

Into a bowl sift together the flour, the ginger, the baking soda, and a pinch of salt. In a small bowl whisk together the egg, the honey, the milk, and the orange zest. In another bowl with an electric mixer beat the butter and the sugar until the mixture is fluffy and add the egg mixture, beating the mixture well. Add the flour mixture and blend the mixture at low speed until it is just combined. Stir in the chocolate chips, drop the batter by rounded tablespoons 2 inches apart onto well-buttered baking sheets, and bake the cookies in a preheated 375° F. oven for 8 to 10 minutes, or until they are golden. Transfer the cookies to racks and let them cool. *The cookies may be kept for 2 days in an airtight container.* Makes about 36 cookies.

184

Poppy Seed Custards

1 tablespoon cornstarch
¾ cup half-and-half
3 tablespoons maple syrup
2 teaspoons poppy seeds, toasted lightly
3 large egg yolks
¼ teaspoon fresh lemon juice

In a small heavy saucepan whisk the cornstarch into ¼ cup of the half-and-half until it is dissolved, whisk in the remaining ½ cup half-and-half, the maple syrup, and the poppy seeds, and cook the mixture over moderately high heat, stirring constantly, until it comes to a boil. Remove the pan from the heat. In a small bowl whisk together the egg yolks, whisk in a little of the hot liquid, and add the yolk mixture to the pan, whisking. Cook the custard over moderate heat, stirring constantly, until it is thickened, being careful not to let it boil. Transfer the custard to a metal bowl set in a bowl of ice and cold water and stir it until it is cool. Whisk in the lemon juice, spoon the custard into two ⅓-cup flameproof soufflé dishes, and broil the custards under a preheated broiler about 2 to 3 inches from the heat for 30 seconds, or until the tops are golden brown. Serves 2.

Zabaglione Mousse

2 large eggs, separated
2 tablespoons sugar
¼ cup Tawny Port
¼ cup well-chilled heavy cream
sliced strawberries for garnish

In a metal bowl set over a saucepan of simmering water combine the egg yolks and the sugar and with an electric mixer beat the mixture at high speed for 5 minutes, or until it is thick and fluffy. Add the Port, 1 tablespoon at a time, beating constantly, and beat the mixture for 3 to 5 minutes, or until it holds soft peaks. Set the metal bowl in a bowl of ice and cold water and beat the mixture for 3 minutes, or until it is cold. In a chilled small bowl beat the cream with the electric mixer until it holds stiff peaks and fold it into the egg yolk mixture. In another bowl beat the egg whites until they hold stiff peaks and fold them into the zabaglione. Spoon the mousse into 2 dessert glasses, chill it for 15 minutes, and serve it immediately, garnished with the strawberries. Serves 2.

Chocolate Apricot Bread Pudding

3 slices of homemade-type white bread
1½ tablespoons unsalted butter, softened
1½ ounces unsweetened chocolate,
  chopped fine
1¼ cups milk
1 large egg
⅓ cup sugar
½ teaspoon vanilla
¼ cup chopped dried apricots
vanilla ice cream as an accompaniment

Spread one side of each slice of bread with the butter and cut the bread into ½-inch pieces. In a small saucepan melt the chocolate in the milk over moderate heat, whisking until the mixture is smooth. In a bowl whisk the egg with the sugar, add the hot milk mixture in a stream, whisking, and stir in the vanilla, the bread pieces, and the apricots. Transfer the mixture to a buttered loaf pan, 9 by 5 by 3 inches, let it stand for 5 minutes, and bake it in the middle of a preheated 375° F. oven for 25 to 30 minutes, or until a knife inserted in the center comes out clean. Serve the bread pudding warm with the ice cream. Serves 2.

Spiced Rice Pudding

¾ cup heavy cream
1¼ cups milk
⅓ cup long-grain rice
1 large whole egg plus 1 large egg yolk,
  beaten lightly
¼ cup sugar
½ teaspoon cinnamon
¼ teaspoon ground cardamom
⅛ teaspoon freshly grated nutmeg
¼ teaspoon vanilla

In a 2-quart heavy saucepan combine the cream and the milk and bring the liquid to a boil. Add the rice and simmer the mixture, covered, stirring occasionally, for 20 minutes, or until the rice is tender. In a bowl whisk together the whole egg and the egg yolk, the sugar, the cinnamon, the cardamom, and the nutmeg, and add ½ cup of the rice mixture, 1 tablespoon at a time, beating. Add the egg mixture to the remaining rice mixture, stirring. Cook the pudding over moderate heat, stirring, for 5 minutes, or until it is thickened, but do not let it boil, and stir in the vanilla. Serves 2.

GENERAL INDEX

S

INDEX OF RECIPES
THAT CAN BE DOUBLED

The recipes listed below can be doubled to serve four people. Throughout the book they are indicated with this symbol: ◆4◆ . Page numbers in italics indicate color photographs.

TABLE SETTING ACKNOWLEDGMENTS

Any items in the photographs not credited are privately owned. All addresses, except where noted, are in New York City.

FRONT JACKET
All items in the photograph are privately owned.

FRONTISPIECE
Chocolate Raspberry Shortcakes (page 2): English pink lusterware dessert plates, circa 1840, and child's cup, circa 1850—Ages Past Antiques, 1030 Lexington Avenue.

THE MENUS
Table Setting (pages 12 and 13): Céralene "Traviata" porcelain dinner plates—Baccarat, Inc., 625 Madison Avenue. Robb & Berking "Alta" sterling flatware—The L•S Collection, 765 Madison Avenue. Water goblets and wineglasses designed by Stephen Smyers; handmade ceramic pitcher and vase by Clarice Cliff, circa 1930—Barneys New York, Seventh Avenue and 17th Street. Hand-painted linen napkins by Liz Wain—Bergdorf Goodman, 754 Fifth Avenue. Bougainvillea trees and anemones—Zezé, 398 East 52nd Street. Fontana Arte glass table; Viaduct "Queen Bess" metal chairs—Modern Age, 41 East 11th Street. Hand-stained wood floor by Veva Crozer—Veva Crozer, 19 Rockwood Lane, Greenwich, Connecticut.

A LIGHT SPRING BRUNCH
Scandinavian Vegetable Soup with Shrimp (page 14): "Dorique" faience plate by Gien from Baccarat, 625 Madison Avenue.

BRUNCH FOR A CHILLY WEEKEND
Sausage and Grits Frittata; Herbed Boston Lettuce and Cherry Tomato Salad (page 16): Italian ceramic dinner plates—Zona, 97 Greene Street. "Polished Stonehenge" stainless-steel flatware; wineglasses—The Pottery Barn, 117 East 59th Street. Hand-painted wood tray—Dean & DeLuca, 560 Broadway.

A ROMANTIC LUNCH
Linguine with Shrimp and Saffron Sauce (page 18): Villeroy & Boch "Medici" porcelain plate; Ricci "Modigliani" silver-plate fork—Mayhew, 507 Park Avenue. Georg Jensen stainless-steel salt and pepper shakers—Avventura, 463 Amsterdam Avenue.

A RAINY DAY LUNCH
Apple Tarts (page 20): Ceramic plates from Portico, 379 West Broadway. French pressed-glass tumblers from Ad Hoc Softwares, 410 West Broadway.

SUMMER HARVEST LUNCHEON
Pasta with Bell Peppers, Goat Cheese, and Basil (page 22): All items in the photograph are privately owned.

LUNCH BEFORE THE GAME
Open-Faced Fried Shrimp Sandwiches with Ginger Mayonnaise (page 24): Ceramic salad plates; "Arlington" glasses—Keesal & Mathews, 1244 Madison Avenue. Bamboo trays (from a set of three); cotton napkin—The Pottery Barn, 117 East 59th Street.

DINNER ON THE PATIO
Grilled Skirt Steak with Parsley Jalapeño Sauce; Brown Buttered Corn with Basil (page 26): Mexican handmade dinner plate and wineglass—Dean & DeLuca, Inc., 560 Broadway. Cotton place mat and napkin by Liz Lauter—Kitchen Classics, Main Street, Bridgehampton, NY.

AN ELEGANT SPRING DINNER
Gingered Poached Apricot and Raspberry Compote (page 28): Carltonware bowls and plate (from a collection of one-of-a-kind pieces), circa 1930—Bergdorf Goodman, 754 Fifth Avenue. Tetard "Marie Antionette" sterling dessert spoon—Cardel, Ltd., 621 Madison Avenue.

A CASUAL SUMMER DINNER
Teriyaki-Style Chicken; Snow Pea and Green Bean Salad (page 30): Ceramic plate—Williams-Sonoma, 20 East 60th Street.

DINNER FOR A SPECIAL OCCASION
Poached Scrod with Herbs and Warm Vinaigrette; Vegetable Ribbons with Horseradish Lemon Butter (page 32): Ceramic plate by Maryse Boxer; hammered flatware—Barneys New York, Seventh Avenue and 17th Street. Wicker tray—The Pottery Barn, 117 East 59th Street.

THE RECIPES
Assorted ingredients (pages 34 and 35): All items in the photograph are privately owned.

STARTERS
Bruschetta with Tomato, Anchovy, and Garlic (page 36): "Tiger" stainless-steel flatware—Conran's Habitat, 160 E. 54th Street. "Antico" hand-made ceramic salad plate—Cottura, (800)348-6608. Cotton placemat and napkin designed by Surface Play—Pier One Imports (all stores).
Lobster-Salad-Stuffed Eggs (page 39): Majolica berry basket (handle not visible),

circa 1900, and plates—Barneys New York, Seventh Avenue and 17th Street.
Sausage and Bell Pepper Hush Puppies with Mustard Sauce (page 41): Chinese cotton place mat; straw basket—The Pottery Barn, 117 East 59th Street.

QUICK BREADS AND PIZZAS
Parmesan Puffs (page 46): English nineteenth-century tole basket—Bob Pryor Antiques, 1023 Lexington Avenue.
Individual Cornmeal Pizzette with Gorgonzola, Escarole, and Bell Pepper (page 54): Hand-thrown and hand-carved stoneware plate by Miranda Thomas; "Provençal" acetal resin and stainless-steel flatware by David Mellor—Simon Pearce, 385 Bleecker Street.

SOUPS
Creamy Lima Bean Soup with Bacon (page 56): Ceramic bowls by Sasaki (each from a 5-piece place setting); cotton napkins and place mats—D.F. Sanders & Co., 952 Madison Avenue. Italian wineglass—from Barneys New York, Seventh Avenue and 17th Street.
Salmon Chowder; Lemon Pepper Crackers (page 62): Nineteenth-century English earthenware soup plate; cotton tablecloth—Cherchez, 862 Lexington Avenue.
Chilled Senegalese Soup with Coriander (page 66): Earthenware soup bowl and plate; acrylic and cotton place mat and napkin—Bergdorf Goodman, 754 Fifth Avenue.

FISH
Marinated Salmon Seared in a Pepper Crust; Creamed Corn and Red Bell Pepper; Tomato, Cucumber, and Feta Salad (page 68): Hand-painted majolica dinner plate designed by Susan Seaberry for Grazia of Deruta, Italy—Kitchen Classics, Main Street, Bridgehampton, NY. Acrylic flatware designed by Laure Japy—Mayhew, 507 Park Avenue. Biot wineglass—Pierre Deux, 870 Madison Avenue.

Sole with Snow Peas and Red Onion in Lemon Vinaigrette (page 73): Mikasa "Harlequin Primary" china dinner plate (from a 20-piece set); metal tray; cotton towel—Bergdorf Goodman, 754 Fifth Avenue.
Sole Paupiettes with Orange Rosemary Butter Sauce (page 75): Italian "Mauresque" ceramic dinner plate; "Jaipur" ceramic dinner fork (from a five-piece place setting); cotton place mat—Thaxton & Company, 780 Madison Avenue.

SHELLFISH
Spicy Steamed Clams with Fennel (page 78): Collection of nineteenth-century Americana—Gail Lettick's Pantry & Hearth Antiques, 121 East 35th Street.
Bell Pepper Filled with Shrimp, Feta, and Pasta Salad (page 87): Hand-thrown earthenware plate by Lyn Evans—Gordon Foster, 1322 Third Avenue.

MEAT
Filets Mignons with Pearl Onions and Artichokes (page 88): Chase Ltd. "Winter Game Birds" porcelain dinner plates—Garfinckel's, 1401 F Street N.W., Washington, D.C. Christofle "Spatours" silver-plate flatware—Pavillon Christofle, 680 Madison Avenue. Italian linen napkin—Frank McIntosh at Henri Bendel, 10 West 57th Street.
Veal Chop "Schnitzel" with Arugula Salad (page 94): Italian earthenware plate and "Bretagne" wineglass—Mayhew, 507 Park Avenue.
Rack of Lamb with Rosemary Scallion Crust; Curried Couscous and Bell Pepper Timbales (page 100): Cartier "La Maison de Cartier" porcelain chop plate—Mayhew, 507 Park Avenue.

POULTRY
Grilled Swiss Cheese and Chicken Sandwiches (page 109): Handmade and hand-painted ceramic plate by Gustavo Gonzalez—Contemporary Porcelain, 105 Sullivan Street.

BREAKFAST, BRUNCH, AND CHEESE DISHES
Corn Waffles with Peppercorn Syrup (page 114): Gien "Arles" faience dinner plate—Avventura, 463 Amsterdam Avenue. Cotton fabric—Pierre Deux, 870 Madison Avenue.
Cheddar Grits Rounds with Ham Hash (page 118): Crown Staffordshire "English Chintz" earthenware platter—Mayhew, 507 Park Avenue.

PASTA
Fusilli with Carrots, Peas, and Mint (page 124): "The Botanic Garden" fine earthenware soup bowl and dinner plate by Portmeirion—Bloomingdale's, 1000 Third Avenue. Glass carafe—Simon Pearce, 385 Bleecker Street.
Linguine with Broccoli Rabe and Lemon (page 129): Ceramic dinner plate; "Carma" silver-plate flatware designed by Izabel Lam; cotton place mat and napkin; wineglass—Frank McIntosh Shop, Henri Bendel, 712 Fifth Avenue.

GRAINS
Baked Polenta with Onions and Bacon (page 141): Cotton jacquard napkins by Primrose Bordier for Le Jacquard Français—Williams-Sonoma, 20 East 60th Street.

VEGETABLES
Cauliflower and Spinach Vinaigrette (page 144): Gien "Holly" faience platter—Baccarat, Inc., 625 Madison Avenue. Hand-painted background by Richard Pellicci, (212) 988-4365 (by appointment only).
Vegetable Pita Pizzas (page 155): Blue glass—The Pottery Barn, 117 East 59th Street.

SALADS
Lentil Salad with Smoked Salmon and Arugula (page 159): French faience dinner plate—Barneys New York, Seventh Avenue and 17th Street.

Lobster Salad with Basil and Lemon Vinaigrette (page 161): Glass plate—Mayhew, 507 Park Avenue.
Tortellini Salad with Arugula (page 167): Handmade earthenware red-leaf dish by Barbara Eigen—Wilder Place, 7975 1/2 Melrose Avenue, Los Angeles, CA 90046.

DESSERTS
Apple Ginger Upside-Down Cake (page 170): Glass cake stand, circa 1900; English nineteenth-century ironstone dessert plate (from a mixed set); glazed cotton napkin— Cherchez, 862 Lexington Avenue.
Lemon Poppy Seed Tea Cakes (page 174): Ceramic platter; cotton napkin—Henri Bendel, Frank McIntosh Shop, 10 West 57th Street.
Gingered Rhubarb with Vanilla Ice Cream (page 181): Blue striped bowl from D.F. Sanders & Co., 386 West Broadway. "Eyelet" hand-painted linen by Ronnie Lasky/Phyllis Heflin—ABC Carpet & Home, 888 Broadway.

BACK JACKET
Linguine with Shrimp and Saffron Sauce: See credits for A Romantic Lunch.
Chocolate Sponge Moons Filled with Peaches and Cream: All items in the photograph are privately owned.
Sole Paupiettes with Orange Rosemary Butter Sauce: See credits for Fish chapter.